I0018323

Advanced JAX-WS Web Services

Practical guide for creating SOAP Web Services using opensource solutions

Alessio Soldano

Advanced JAX-WS Web Services

ISBN 978-88-94038910

ISBN 978-88-940389-1-0 90000

9 788894 038910

Preface

Web Services technologies have been around for a lot of years. The standardization process of XML-based Web Services APIs within the Java Platform started more then a decade ago with JAX-RPC (JSR 101), and it was 2006 when the Standard Edition of Java Platform (JDK 6) eventually included a standard and mature API for dealing with Web Services, JAX-WS (JSR 224). Nowadays, despite both the technologies and the relevant Java API being well consolidated and thoroughly used, some users still find the learning curve for this topic quite steep. First time users need a guide leading them from the Web Services theory and standard specifications to actual Java API usage in their development environment, while coping with advanced business requirements (for instance in terms of security). The aim of this book is hence to provide practical advices on building and deploying Web Services applications in the enterprise. Starting from the basics and the best practices for setting up a development environment, this book enters into most of JAX-WS inner details in a clear and concise way. For those targetting WildFly as application server container, the book also features step-by-step development and deployment directions as well as advanced configuration details; this allows user to get the best from the container and avoid common pitfalls and mistakes with web services applications. Finally, an advanced topic like Web Services security is covered, showing users how to actually leverage modern policy-based Web Services standards to deal with authentication, authorization, message integrity and message confidentiality.

The Author of the Book

Alessio Soldano was born in Varese, Italy in 1979 and graduated with a degree in Computer Science Engineering from 'Politecnico di Milano'. After having worked for some years on distributed systems in the financial/credit field, he joined JBoss / Red Hat at the end of 2007. Since then, he's been working full time on the webservice project, currently serving as its lead. He also contributes to WildFly and other JBoss projects. Starting from 2009, Alessio
represents Red Hat Middleware on JSR-224 'JavaTM API for XML-Based Web Services (JAX-WS) 2.0' expert group. Alessio has also represented Red Hat at the W3C Web Services Resource Access Working Group. Finally, Alessio is committer and PMC member of the Apache CXF webservice project.

4

The reviewers

Francesco Marchioni is an OpenGroup and Sun Certified Enterprise Architect living in Rome. He has joined the JBoss community in early 2000 when the application server was a mere EJB container, running release 2.x. Since 2009, he is ruuning an IT portal focused on JBoss products (http://www.mastertheboss.com) which is pleased to serve an average of 8000 daily visits.

He has published several successful book titles at PacktPublishing and ItBuzzPress.

What this book covers

Chapter 1: First steps with JAX-WS Web Services, discusses about what JAX-WS is and how to get started with developing services using it.

Chapter 2: Developing JAX-WS Web Service Applications, dives deep into Web Services development. In particular, you will get detailed information on how to create Web Service clients from a WSDL contract, how to create a full Web Service project using the WSDL-to-Java tools and top-down methodology. Finally, we will show another option for creating a full Web Service project using a Maven archetype specifically focused on WildFly

Chapter 3: Advanced JAX-WS and JAXB usage, covers some advanced concepts that are often required to deal with non trivial web services applications such as Oneway invocations, JAX-WS handlers, JavaEE injection and JAX-WS components, Asynchronous invocations, Fault handling

Chapter 4: WildFly JAX-WS Provider, provides information on how the JAX-WS specification is implemented in WildFly. While users can certainly rely on the vanilla WildFly configuration, a good grasp of the various layers building up the Web Services stack of the server allows better configuration and tuning.

Chapter 5: Web Services Security, introduces to the most common concerns about Web Services security. After an initial overview of the key security concepts some common scenarios will be described through source code examples and directions on configuring the WildFly container properly.

Appendix: Shows how to create top-down Web Services and Web Service clients using the Eclipse wizard. Detailed instructions on running tests are included.

Trademarks

JBoss ® is a registered trademark of RedHat Inc. in US and other countries. Apache CXF ® is a registered trademark of The Apache Software Foundation.

Source code of this book

This book contains quite a lot of code. You can find the book's examples at Github:
https://github.com/asoldano/jaxws-book

Feel free to provide updates to the examples. If the updates improve the quality of the examples, we will certainly include them in the main repository.

Who this book is for

This book is especially suited for Java Developers, Architects and Testers that make use of service-oriented solutions based on Web Services. This book will help you to understand the most common challenges of developing XML-based (SOAP) Web Services using opensource solutions such as WildFly application server and Apache CXF libraries. We have included as well some general Web Service exposure, which will help you to run the examples contained in this book on other popular containers such as Tomcat or Glassfish.

How to Contact Us

Please address comments and questions concerning this book to the publisher:

info@itbuzzpress.com . We have created a web page for this book, where we list errata, examples, and any other information. You can access this page at: http://www.itbuzzpress.com/news/jax-ws-errata.html

For more information about our books, and future projects see our website at:
http://www.itbuzzpress.com

Piracy

The uploading/downloading of copyrighted material without the express written consent of the content copyright holder is strictly forbidden. Piracy is an illegal act that you may aspire to reconsider. Besides this, piracy is not a victimless crime! It is financially damaging and personally hurtful to company employees and their families. Legitimate users suffer as well. We appreciate your help in protecting the valuable content of this book.

"To Arianna, my daughter"

Index

Chapter 1: First steps with JAX-WS Web Services

This chapter discusses about what **JAX-WS** is and how to get started with developing services using it. The focus of the book will mainly be on **JBossWS** a Web Service framework developed as part of **WildFly** (formerly known as JBoss Application Server), that implements the JAX-WS specification (JSR 224, Java API for XML-based Web Services 2.0). Most of what will be explained, especially in this chapter, still applies to any JAX-WS implementation, though.

You will get your hands on the following topics:

- A short introduction to Web Services

- How to easily create your first Web Service endpoint

- How to build and deploy Web Services applications (using Maven directly or IDEs)

JAX-WS Overview

JAX-WS is a Java API for producing and consuming SOAP-style web services. It is defined by the JSR-224 specification from the Java Community Process (JCP). It is actually possible to build also REST-style Web Services with JAX-WS (using @WebServiceProvider annotated classes), but that's not the main goal of JAX-WS.

JAX-WS is the successor of **JAX-RPC**, an API for XML-based remote procedure call (RPC). The Reference Implementation (RI) for JAX-WS is part of the open source GlassFish project and is named **Metro**. The current version of JAX-WS is 2.2.x. JAX-WS is officially part of Java Enterprise Edition (Java EE) and is included in JDK since version 1.6.

JAX-WS endpoints can be published on any Java EE compliant application server (or at least implementing the JSR 224 specification); those include for instance WildFly, GlassFish, JBoss EAP, etc. It is also possible to publish JAX-WS endpoints on Servlet containers (like Tomcat) as well as on many HTTP servers (such as Jetty, Grizzly, Undertow) using the convenient **Endpoint Publisher** API.

Besides the Metro reference implementation, there are multiple alternatives for building JAX-WS services; the most known ones are Apache CXF and Apache Axis2, which are also leveraged by some JavaEE containers to offer Web Services functionality.

The JAX-WS implementation in WildFly comes from JBossWS, a Web Services Framework, which also implements JSR-109. JBossWS internally bundles most components of Apache CXF and provides additional functionalities and customized tooling.

Each vendor specific implementation usually adds features and configuration options to the plain JAX-WS API; however as long as the user sticks with standard JAX-WS API usage only, web services applications should be easily portable into a different container relying on a different -yet compliant- JAX-WS implementation.

Moreover JAX-WS uses standard technologies defined by W3C (such as SOAP or WSDL), which control the messages' format, the way of describing published services, etc. Therefore, any JAX-WS endpoint can be invoked by proper clients developed with different frameworks or programming language.

JAX-WS Architecture

Web Services are described using the standard **Web Service Description Language (WSDL)**. This means one or more XML files containing information on the service location (endpoint address), service functionalities (operations), input/output messages involved in the communication and business data structure (usually in the form of one or more XML Schema definition). Recent specifications (like WS-Policy) allow more advanced service capabilities to be stated in the contract through WSDL extensions.

The communication between endpoints (described using WSDL) and clients is standardized by the **SOAP** specification; SOAP defines the envelope structure, encoding rules, and conventions for representing web service invocation and response XML messages.

The JAX-WS API hides the complexity of WSDL and SOAP from the application developer. On the server side, the developer specifies the web service operations by defining methods in an interface written in the Java programming language. The developer also provides classes implementing that interface according to existing business rules.

On client side, the developer uses a proxy (a local object representing the service) on which methods are invoked to call the corresponding web service operation. Hence, the developer does not generate or parse SOAP messages *directly*. The developer deals with Java classes that are internally marshalled to and unmarshalled from SOAP messages by the JAX-WS runtime.

Of course, JAX-WS implementations come with tools for automatically generating client proxies as well as initial endpoint interfaces given a WSDL contract. Similarly, WSDL documents can be automatically created given a web service endpoint implementation.

Finally, a note on marshalling / unmarshalling of input / output messages: when processing contracts, JAX-WS tools map WSDL operations and bindings to web service interface methods. The arguments for such methods might be described by complex types in the WSDL, perhaps imported from external schemas. The mapping is performed using an available implementation of **JAXB** (Java API for XML Binding). In few words, Java classes with JAXB annotations are **automatically mapped** to schema types defined in the WSDL contract. At runtime, JAX-WS relies on JAXB for mapping the instances of such classes to actual message payloads to be used in the generated SOAP messages.

Software you need to install

In order to be able to run our examples, there are some initial requirements, which need to be satisfied on your machine. The following section contains the list of software and tools which you need to install.

Java Development Kit

As we will code our Web Services endpoints in Java, we obviously need a Java Virtual Machine available. The Java SDK can be downloaded from the following link:
http://www.oracle.com/technetwork/pt/java/javase/downloads/index.html

There are several version of Java available. If you are running a Windows machine, you will need to download an executable installer. If you are running Linux machine, you can opt for other alternatives. In this case, I will be using the RPM version on a Red Hat Linux operating system.

After you download Java, we can now begin the Java installation. Use the following commands on a root shell:

```
[root@alessio ~]# rpm -ivh jdk-7u45-linux-x64.rpm
```

After installation, we must set the **JAVA_HOME** environment variable in /etc/profile :

```
export JAVA_HOME="/usr/java/jdk1.7.0_45"
export PATH="$PATH:$JAVA_HOME/bin"
```

Now run the command below to apply the new configuration:

```
[root@alessio ~]# source /etc/profile
```

To check the integrity of the installation, just run a simple Java command to verify:

```
[root@alessio ~]# java -version
java version "1.7.0_45"
Java(TM) SE Runtime Environment (build 1.7.0_45-b18)
Java HotSpot(TM) 64-Bit Server VM (build 24.45-b08, mixed mode)
```

With the Java installation successfully completed, we are now able to move to the next topic.

WildFly application server

JAX-WS Web Services can be executed on any Java EE compatible container; we will however choose the WildFly application server as main reference for our examples. Later on in this chapter, we will provide instructions for running our first Web Service on other containers such as Tomcat or Glassfish.

WildFly 8 can be downloaded from http://www.wildfly.org by following the Downloads link in the home page, which will take you to the following screen:

Version	Date	Description	License	Size	Format
8.1.0.Final	2014-05-30	Java EE7 Full & Web Distribution	LGPL	124 MB	⬇ ZIP
				111 MB	⬇ TGZ
		Update Existing 8.0.0.Final Install	LGPL	110 MB	⬇ ZIP
		Minimalistic Core Distribution	LGPL	15 MB	⬇ ZIP
		Application Server Source Code	LGPL	30 MB	⬇ ZIP

Once downloaded, extract the archive to a folder and you are done with the installation:

```
unzip wildfly-8.1.0.Final.zip
```

Maven

Creating Java EE applications can be done in a variety of ways. Most developers can begin with quickstarts and demo contained in Eclipse or NetBeans environment. Nevertheless, as your application grows in complexity, so does the amount of libraries to be used (and especially the dependencies between them). For this reason, you are strongly encouraged to use **Maven** that is the *de facto* standard tool for project and release management. Maven is distributed in several formats and can be downloaded from this link: http://maven.apache.org/download.html

Once you have completed the download, unzip the distribution archive (for example, apache-maven-3.2.1-bin.zip) in the directory where you wish to install Maven.

Next, add the *M2_HOME* environment variable to your system, so that it will point to the folder where Maven has been unpacked. Next, update the *PATH* environment variable by adding the Maven binaries to your system path. For example, on the Windows platform, you should include *%M2_HOME%/bin*, to make Maven available to the command line.

Once completed with your installation, run mvn --version, to verify that Maven has been correctly installed:

```
mvn --version
Apache Maven 3.2.1 ( 2014-02-14T18:37:52+01:00)
Maven home: C:\apache-maven-3.2.1\bin\..
Java version: 1.7.0_55, vendor: Oracle Corporation
Java home: C:\Java\jdk1.7.0_55\jre
```

Creating a simple Web Service endpoint with JAX-WS

Once that you have installed all the required tools, we can start building our first Web Service endpoint. Actually, multiple approaches actually exist for Web Service development, which can be grouped in two broad categories:

- **Top-down Web Services**: means that you start with a Web Service definition (described in the WSDL) and then create all the necessary scaffolding in Java all the way down.

- **Bottom-up Web Services**: means you start with a Java class and generate the WSDL from it.

We will start by the latter approach, which is the simplest choice for a developer, whilst we will defer top-down Web Services in the next chapter.

Bottom-up Web Service endpoints

The first and most straightforward approach for developing a Web Service endpoint (**bottom-up**) is to rely on an existing **Java Bean** (POJO, Plain Old Java Object); that could be part of the application business logic or written from scratch for the sake of creating the Web Service endpoint. The bean can be easily turned into a Web Service Endpoint Implementation by properly annotating it.

This approach is usually the preferred one when existing business components need to be made available as Web Service endpoints too and there's no actual requirement on the contract that will be published for them.

 On containers supporting the full JavaEE specification set (for instance WildFly), EJB 3 beans can be annotated the same way as POJOs and exposed as Web Service endpoint.

Our Web Service will be included in a Java EE 7 Web project; hence, it will be deployed as part of a Web application. Both Eclipse and NetBeans have some wizards to create some initial Web application projects: as we will choose a vanilla approach, based on Maven, we can create our initial project named **ws-demo**, which is derived from the **webapp-javaee7** archetype:

So from a command prompt execute the following shell:

```
mvn -DarchetypeGroupId=org.codehaus.mojo.archetypes -DarchetypeArtifactId=webapp-javaee7 -
DarchetypeVersion=0.4-SNAPSHOT -
DarchetypeRepository=https://nexus.codehaus.org/content/repositories/snapshots -
DgroupId=com.itbuzzpress.chapter1 -DartifactId=ws-demo -Dversion=1.0 -
Dpackage=com.itbuzzpress.chapter1 -Darchetype.interactive=false --batch-mode --update-
snapshots archetype:generate
```

The following structure will be generated in a folder named ws-demo:

```
$ tree ws-demo
├───src
    └───main
        ├───java
        │   └───com
        │       └───itbuzzpress
        │           └───chapter1
        └───webapp
            └───WEB-INF
```

Now, we will add our first Web Service endpoint, named **HelloWorld** under the
src/main/java/com/itbuzzpress/chapter1 folder:

```
package com.itbuzzpress.chapter1;
import javax.jws.*;

@WebService
public class HelloWorld {
   @WebMethod
   public String echo(String input) {
      return "Hi "+input;
   }
}
```

As you can see, this basic Web Service contains an annotation within it, named
@javax.jws.WebService. Java Beans annotated, with *@WebService* end up being exposed as endpoints
once the application they're included in is deployed on a target container supporting JAX-WS. At
deployment time, the container processes the annotated beans and generates the WSDL document
describing the service contract.

The *@WebService* annotation actually has some optional attributes to control the published contract, as
well as to specify an endpoint interface. An explicit endpoint interface is used to clearly state the
methods that are to be part of the service contract, perhaps when the bean is quite complex.

The *javax.jws.WebMethod* annotation can be used on both endpoint bean and interface methods to
tell the container to include them in the service contract. All method parameters and return types
must either be simple Java types or be compatible with the JAXB 2 specification.

There are sensible defaults for all the JSR-181 annotations, defining the container behavior when
they're not used.

 A Java Bean is exposed as Web Service endpoint by annotating it with
javax.jws.WebService or *javax.jws.WebServiceProvider*. *@WebServiceProvider* lets users
directly define the SOAP messages to be exchanged by the endpoint, bypassing the
container marshalling/unmarshalling of JAXB style classes used as method
parameters.

Building, Packaging and Deploying the Service

A relevant aspect of web services application development is how to build, package and deploy them. Different target containers come with different requirements on the deployment archive to provide, which affects the way applications are to be built and packaged. However, there are common steps and requirements for creating proper deployments containing JAX-WS endpoints. Below you find some directions on the main aspect regarding packaging:

Deployment type

Different containers have different requirements on the kind of archive to produce. On Java EE compliant containers, JAR or WAR archives are expected, depending on the type of endpoints which are included (POJO Web Service endpoints are to be packaged into WAR archives whilst EJB endpoints can be packaged as well in JAR archives).

Deployment contents

In terms of which class files to include, a JAX-WS endpoint deployment must contain the web **Service Endpoint Implementation** class and its interface (if any), as well as any class used for operation parameters and results.

Some containers may require portable JAX-WS artifacts to be generated and included in the deployment, by running a **java-to-wsdl tool** if the endpoint has been developed following a bottom-up approach. Those artifacts usually include the generated WSDL for the endpoint interface, as well as request and response wrapper classes (which are needed by containers for some type of contracts).

The JAX-WS 2.2 specification allows endpoints to be discovered in the deployment even if no descriptor is provided (as a matter of fact WAR archives can have no *web.xml)*. If included, the content of the *web.xml* file, as well as any additional descriptor, depends on the actual target container where the archive is meant to be deployed.

 When it comes to WildFly, no additional java-to-wsdl tool run is required, as the container will process the deployment contents at runtime and automatically generates any needed wrapper class as well as the published WSDL document.

Building and packaging with Maven

Since we have created our project with Maven, we will use it for building up and packaging the Web Service contained in it. The *pom.xml* which has been generated by the archetype:generate method is quite verbose so we will not include all its sections here (You can inspect for the source code of this example on GitHub at: https://github.com/asoldano/jaxws-book/tree/master/chapter1/ws-demo)

The most relevant section of it, is contained at the beginning of the *pom.xml* file:

```
<project xmlns="http://maven.apache.org/POM/4.0.0"
xmlns:xsi="http://www.w3.org/2001/XMLSchema-instance"
xsi:schemaLocation="http://maven.apache.org/POM/4.0.0 http://maven.apache.org/xsd/maven-4.0.0.xsd">
    <modelVersion>4.0.0</modelVersion>
    <groupId>com.itbuzzpress.chapter1</groupId>
    <artifactId>ws-demo</artifactId>
    <version>1.0</version>
    <packaging>war</packaging>
    <name>ws-demo</name>
    <properties>
        <endorsed.dir>${project.build.directory}/endorsed</endorsed.dir>
        <project.build.sourceEncoding>UTF-8</project.build.sourceEncoding>
    </properties>


    <dependencies>
        <dependency>
            <groupId>javax</groupId>
            <artifactId>javaee-web-api</artifactId>
            <version>7.0</version>
            <scope>provided</scope>
        </dependency>
    </dependencies>
......
```

As you can see from the packaging element, war (Web application archive) will be generated by packaging this application. The only dependency included in this example is the javaee-web-api. Please note *provided* dependency scope is selected, as the dependency is not meant to be transitive and, very important, is not to be included in the application archive produced by the build.

As we are not including any API in our application, we rely on the **server classloader** to load the JAX-WS API implementation available on the server side. Conversely, on Web Service client applications, the Maven project dependencies concur in defining the classpath the application classloader is derived from. It is hence critical to verify which JAX-WS implementation is pulled in by the specified dependencies.

If no JAX-WS implementation is transitively pulled by the specified dependencies, the JAX-WS reference implementation included in the JDK is used.

A Maven project described by the above *pom.xml* and including the sources as per Maven conventions (following the Maven standard directory layout), is built simply running the following command:

```
mvn clean package
```

Deploying the application

The target application archive is finally to be deployed to the target container. This is achieved differently depending on the actual selected container.

On WildFly multiple deploy mechanisms are available, but the most straightforward one is probably to hot deploy the WAR archive by copying it into the *standalone/deployment* folder of the server instance.

```
$ cp ws-demo-1.0.war /usr/share/wildfly-8.1.0.Final/standalone/deployments
```

The application server will now start deploying your application and activate the Web Service endpoint, as it's evident from the following log:

```
Adding service endpoint metadata: id=com.itbuzzpress.chapter1.HelloWorld
  address=http://localhost:8080/ws-demo-1.0/HelloWorld
  implementor=com.itbuzzpress.chapter1.HelloWorld
  serviceName={http://chapter1.itbuzzpress.com/}HelloWorldService
  portName={http://chapter1.itbuzzpress.com/}HelloWorldPort
  annotationWsdlLocation=null
```

You can check that the WSDL has been correctly generated by opening the Administration console of the application server, which is available by default at the following address: http://localhost:9990

Web Service Endpoints

Web Service Endpoints. Endpoints need to be deployed as regular applications.

Available Web Service Endpoints

▲ Name	Context	Deployment
com.itbuzzpress.chapter1.HelloWorld	ws-demo-1.0	ws-demo-1.0.war

Name:	com.itbuzzpress.chapter1.HelloWorld
Context:	ws-demo-1.0
Class:	com.itbuzzpress.chapter1.HelloWorld
Type:	JAXWS_JSE
WSDL Url:	http://localhost:8080/ws-demo-1.0/HelloWorld?wsdl
Deployment:	ws-demo-1.0.war

Testing the application

In order to test a Web Service there are many available options: you can either code a Web Service client in your favorite language (Java, PHP, Ruby etc.) or use a tool for testing your Web Service endpoints. We will choose at first the latter option, that is installing a testing tool, whilst next chapter will focus on creating native Java Web Service clients.

The tool that we will use for this purpose is **SoapUI** (http://www.soapui.org/) which is a popular User Interface for testing SOAP based Web Services, although it is able as well to act as a client for RESTFul Web Services and much more. SoapUI is available both as standalone application and as Eclipse Plugin. The downloads of SoapUI Community version are hosted on SourceForge at: http://sourceforge.net/projects/soapui/files/ .

Once that you have installed the version which is appropriate with your system, launch SoapUI. From the **File** Menu select **New SOAP Project**.

21

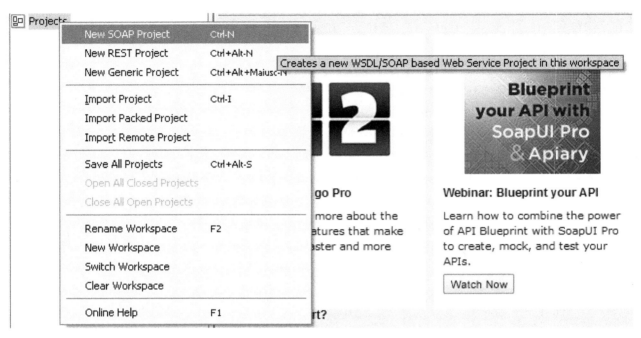

This will open a New SOAP Project dialog. In the **Initial WSDL** field, enter the location where the WSDL contract is contained, as displayed by the following picture:

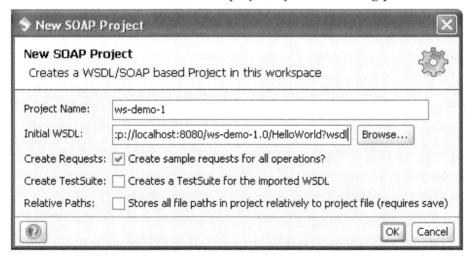

Click **OK**. You should now see that the WSDL was successfully added to the project by seeing the operations in the Web Service in the navigator.

Double click on the **Request1** tree element: the **soapUI Request** Perspective will appear where you can fill up the named parameters:

```
http://localhost:8080/ws-demo-1.0/HelloWorld

<soapenv:Envelope xmlns:soapenv="http://schemas.xmlsoap.org/so
    <soapenv:Header/>
    <soapenv:Body>
        <chap:echo>
            <!--Optional:-->
            <arg0>Alessio</arg0>
        </chap:echo>
    </soapenv:Body>
</soapenv:Envelope>
```

In the corresponding Response Window, you will check the result of your Web Service invocation:

```xml
<soap:Envelope xmlns:soap="http://schemas.xmlsoap.org/soap/envelope/">
    <soap:Body>
        <ns2:echoResponse xmlns:ns2="http://chapter1.itbuzzpress.com/">
            <return>Hi Alessio</return>
        </ns2:echoResponse>
    </soap:Body>
</soap:Envelope>
```

As you can see, we successfully tested our first Web Service deployed on WildFly server.

Exposing EJB 3 as Web Services

So far, we have seen how you can promote your Java classes to Web Services by merely adding some annotations at the class level; however, the JAX-WS specification also allows exposing a Stateless Session Bean as Web Services almost in the same way you would do with a POJO.

Here is for example, how you can expose the initial example as Stateless EJB:

```java
package com.itbuzzpress.chapter1;
import javax.jws.WebMethod;
import javax.jws.WebService;
import javax.ejb.Stateless;


@WebService
@Stateless
public class HelloWorld {
   @WebMethod
   public String echo(String input) {
      return "Hi "+input;
   }
}
```

Although being quite similar to the POJO counterpart, using EJB 3 as endpoint has some peculiarities: for example you can use annotations to define both the **Context Root** and the **Url Pattern** that will be use to bind the Web Service. In the former example, we could set:

```
@WebService
@WebContext( contextRoot = "/webservices" , urlPattern="/HelloWorldService" )
@Stateless
public class HelloWorld {

. . .

}
```

In the above example, when deploying the Web Service endpoint, we would bind it to
http://locallhost:8080/webservices/HelloWorldService

Building and packaging JAX-WS services on other Containers

Coding a Web Service using JAX-WS is a portable choice that will let you run your Web Service on most Java containers (such as Tomcat or Glassfish). On the other hand, when porting your Web Service application to Servlet container such as Tomcat, you need a different procedure for building and packaging your application; actually, Apache Tomcat does not ship with a JAX-WS implementation, therefore the following steps are required in order to deploy your Web Service.

1. At first you need to pack along with your application a valid **JAX-WS implementation**. The most straightforward solution is to rely on the JAX-WS Reference Implementation (RI), which is available at: https://jax-ws.java.net/ . The libraries need to be bundled in the WEB-INF/lib folder of your application deployment; when using Maven for building the application, that is usually simply achieved by declaring the following dependency in the project's *pom.xml*:

```
<dependencies>
        <dependency>
            <groupId>com.sun.xml.ws</groupId>
            <artifactId>jaxws-rt</artifactId>
            <version>2.1.3</version>
        </dependency>
</dependencies>
```

2. Next, in the *web.xml* descriptor of your application, you need to declare a **ServletListener class,** which parses the Sun's RI configuration file, *sun-jaxws.xml*.

```
<web-app>
      <listener>
            <listener-class>
                  com.sun.xml.ws.transport.http.servlet.WSServletContextListener
            </listener-class>
      </listener>
      <servlet>
            <servlet-name>echo</servlet-name>
            <servlet-class>
                  com.sun.xml.ws.transport.http.servlet.WSServlet
            </servlet-class>
            <load-on-startup>1</load-on-startup>
      </servlet>
      <servlet-mapping>
            <servlet-name>echo</servlet-name>
            <url-pattern>/echo</url-pattern>
      </servlet-mapping>
</web-app>
```

3. Finally, a *sun-jaxws.xml* file has to be included within the *WEB-INF* folder of your Web application:

```
<endpoints xmlns="http://java.sun.com/xml/ns/jax-ws/ri/runtime"
      version="2.0">
      <endpoint name="HelloWorld"
            implementation="com.itbuzzpress.chapter1.HelloWorld"
            url-pattern="/echo" />
</endpoints>
```

The above file defines the Service Endpoint Implementation class as the endpoint of your project, along with the URL pattern of the Web Service.

Once the application has been packaged, it can be deployed to the Web container using the available management instruments. On Tomcat, you can simply drop the Web application in the *webapps* folder to start the deployment procedure.

When deploying the Web Service to Apache Tomcat you need to specify the **SOAP Binding** to be used (DOCUMENT or RPC) on the Web Service, as indicated in the following snippet:

```
@WebService
@SOAPBinding(style = Style.RPC)
public class HelloWorld    {

  . . . .

}
```

Actually, using the **@SOAPBinding** annotation is optional, because if not specified it defaults to the DOCUMENT. However, the Tomcat deployer will issue an error if you fail to specify the SOAPBinding.

The main difference between **DOCUMENT** and **RPC** is that a DOCUMENT invocation can be fully validated by a standard validating XML parser, while an RPC invocation cannot because of the implied wrapper element around the invocation body.

Chapter 2: Developing JAX-WS Web Service Applications

This chapter dives deep into Web Services development. In particular, you will get detailed information on the following topics:

- At first we will learn how to create Web Service clients from a WSDL contract

- Next we will show how to create a full Web Service project using the WSDL-to-Java tools and top-down methodology

- Finally, we will show another option for creating a full Web Service project using a Maven archetype specifically focused on WildFly

A step-by-step procedure for coding, building, deploying and testing our Web Service enabled applications will eventually be provided.

A Simple JAX-WS Application Client

In the first chapter, we have learnt how to test Web Services using a tool named SoapUI. Now it's time to learn how to code Web Services using native Java clients. Web Service clients are usually created by starting from an existing WSDL contract. Most of the JAX-WS implementations come with tools to generate the required JAX-WS artifacts to build the client. Below the **JBossWS tools** will be used, but similar commands exist for other tools; it is recommended to check the manual for the specific tool being used.

wsconsume is the JBossWS **wsdl-to-java** tool and is available in different flavors: as a command line script, as Ant task and as a Maven plugin. The command line script is located in the *bin* folder of the WildFly distribution; hence, you can include this folder in your System Path in order to execute it from any file system location:

```
export PATH=$JBOSS_HOME/bin:$PATH
```

In the following example, the wsconsume script is used to consume a local copy of a WSDL contract to generate a Web Service client; an URL to the remote location where the contract is published could have also been used as well.

```
$ ./wsconsume.sh -k CustomerService.wsdl
```

The specified WSDL document (available at https://github.com/asoldano/jaxws-book/tree/master/chapter2) is processed by the tool and portable JAX-WS artifacts are generated. The table below describes them:

File	Description
Customer.java	The **Service Endpoint Interface**: a @WebService annotated interface describing the service
CustomerService.java	The **Service Factory** class: a @WebServiceClient annotated class extending javax.xml.ws.Service
USAddress.java, CustomerRecord.java	JAXB annotated classes for the custom data types defined in the contract.
ObjectFactory.java, package-info.java	JAXB support classes. The package-info.java is a Java file that can be added to any Java source package. Its purpose is to provide a home for package level documentation and package level annotations.

Web Service clients make use of service stubs that hide the details of a remote Web Service invocation; to a client application, a WS invocation looks like just an invocation of any other business component. In this case, the generated service endpoint interface acts as the business interface. The generated **Service Factory** is used by JAX-WS to present the service stub as an implementation of the endpoint interface.

Therefore, when you are coding your Web Service client you need to create an instance of the **Service Factory** (CustomerService). The simplest way to do that is using the constructor with no parameters, which creates an instance referencing the local WSDL document specified when running the tools.

```
CustomerService service = new CustomerService();
```

If you have a look at the CustomerService class, you will see that there are also other constructors available for creating an instance of the Service Factory:

```java
public class CustomerService extends Service {

public final static URL WSDL_LOCATION;
public final static QName SERVICE = new QName("http://foo.org/", "CustomerService");
public final static QName CustomerPort = new QName("http://foo.org/", "CustomerPort");

public CustomerService(URL wsdlLocation) {
    super(wsdlLocation, SERVICE);
}

public CustomerService(URL wsdlLocation, QName serviceName) {
    super(wsdlLocation, serviceName);
}

public CustomerService() {
    super(WSDL_LOCATION, SERVICE);
}

public CustomerService(WebServiceFeature ... features) {
    super(WSDL_LOCATION, SERVICE, features);
}

public CustomerService(URL wsdlLocation, WebServiceFeature ... features) {
    super(wsdlLocation, SERVICE, features);
}
```

```
public CustomerService(URL wsdlLocation, QName serviceName, WebServiceFeature ... features)
{
    super(wsdlLocation, serviceName, features);
}
```

The constructor accepting a *wsdlLocation URL* parameter can be used to specify a different location for the contract, perhaps because at runtime that is available elsewhere. Similarly, the service *QName* can be specified (useful for contracts having multiple WSDL services). Finally, additional *WebServiceFeature* parameters can be provided, for tuning the client stub creation on JAX-WS implementations supporting additional configurations.

Once the Service Factory is created, the **CustomerService** class provides a way to obtain a stub, which is implementing the **Service Interface**. This can be done using one of the *@WebEndpoint* annotated methods of the factory:

```
@WebEndpoint(name = "CustomerPort")
public Customer getCustomerPort() {
    return super.getPort(CustomerPort, Customer.class);
}

@WebEndpoint(name = "CustomerPort")
public Customer getCustomerPort(WebServiceFeature... features) {
    return super.getPort(CustomerPort, Customer.class, features);
}
```

The optional *WebServiceFeature* parameters allow controlling the way the stub is created and configured; standard features exist for enabling MTOM and WS-Addressing.

A minimal client for the endpoint described by the consumed contract would hence look as follows:

```
CustomerService service = new CustomerService();
Customer port = service.getCustomerPort();
CustomerRecord record = port.locateCustomer("John", "Li", null);
USAddress address = record.getAddress();
```

Besides for the customizations mentioned above, please note that it's also possible to write a more dynamic client, which is not bound to the generated service factory. That is achieved by directly using the *javax.xml.ws.Service* class:

```
import javax.xml.ws.Service;


Service service = Service.create(new URL("http://foo.org/service?wsdl"), new
Qname("http://foo.org/", "CustomerService"));

Customer port = service.getPort(new QName("http://foo.org/", "CustomerPort",
Customer.class);
[...]
```

 The namespaces and local names in the QName objects provided to get the client stub need to match the actual *name* attributes of *{http://schemas.xmlsoap.org/wsdl/}service* and *{http://schemas.xmlsoap.org/wsdl/}portType* elements in the WSDL.

Any parameter to the service interface methods, as well as any return type, is going to be a simple Java type or one of the generated and JAXB annotated classes.

So the client can invoke the remote service endpoint as if it was a local bean.

Developing a top-down Web Service project

The **bottom-up** approach for creating a Web Service endpoint has been introduced in the first chapter. It allows exposing existing beans as Web Service endpoints very quickly: in most cases, turning the classes into endpoints is a matter of simply adding few annotations in the code.

However, when developing a service with an already defined contract, it is far simpler (and effective) to use the **top-down** approach, since a **wsdl-to-java** tool can generate the annotated code matching the WSDL. This is the preferred solution in multiple scenarios such as the following ones:

- Creating a service that adheres to the XML Schema and WSDL that have been developed by hand up front;

- Exposing a service that conforms to a contract specified by a third party (e.g. a vendor that calls the service using an already defined set of messages);

- Replacing the implementation of an existing Web Service while keeping compatibility with older clients (the contract must not change).

In the next sections, an example of **top-down** Web Service endpoint development is provided, as well as some details on constraints the developer has to be aware of when coding, regardless of the chosen approach.

Creating a Web Service using the top-down approach

In order to set up a full project which includes a Web Service endpoint and a JAX-WS client we will use two Maven projects. The first one will be a standard webapp-javaee7 project, which will contain the Web Service Endpoint. The second one, will be just a quickstart Maven project that will execute a Test case against the Web Service.

Let's start creating the server project as usual with:

```
mvn -DarchetypeGroupId=org.codehaus.mojo.archetypes -DarchetypeArtifactId=webapp-javaee7 -
DarchetypeVersion=0.4-SNAPSHOT -
DarchetypeRepository=https://nexus.codehaus.org/content/repositories/snapshots -
DgroupId=com.itbuzzpress.chapter2.wsdemo -DartifactId=ws-demo2 -Dversion=1.0 -
Dpackage=com.itbuzzpress.chapter2.wsdemo -Darchetype.interactive=false --batch-mode --
update-snapshots archetype:generate
```

Next step will be creating the Web Service interface and stubs from a WSDL contract. The steps are similar to those for building up a client for the same contract. The only difference is that the *wsconsume* script will output the generated source files into our Maven project:

```
$ wsconsume.bat -k CustomerService.wsdl -o ws-demo-wsdl\src\main\java
```

In addition to the generated classes, which we have discussed at the beginning of the chapter, we need to provide a **Service Endpoint Implementation** that contains the Web Service functionalities:

```
@WebService(endpointInterface="org.jboss.test.ws.jaxws.samples.webresult.Customer")
public class CustomerImpl implements Customer {
    public CustomerRecord locateCustomer(String firstName, String lastName, USAddress
address) {
        CustomerRecord cr = new CustomerRecord();
        cr.setFirstName(firstName);
        cr.setLastName(lastName);
        return cr;
    }
}
```

The endpoint implementation class implements the endpoint interface and references it through the *@WebService* annotation. Our WebService class does nothing fancy, just create a CustomerRecord object using the parameters received as input. In a real world example, you would collect the CustomerRecord using the Persistence Layer for example.

Once the implementation class has been included in the project, the project needs to be packaged and deployed to the target container, which will expose the service endpoint with the same contract that was consumed by the tool.

 It is also possible to reference a local WSDL file in the *@WebService* **wsdlLocation** attribute in the Service Interface and include the file in the deployment. That would make the exact provided document be published.

Requirements of a JAX-WS endpoint

Regardless of the approach chosen for developing a JAX-WS endpoint, the actual implementation needs to satisfy some requirements:

- The implementing class must be annotated with either the *javax.jws.WebService* or the *javax.jws.WebServiceProvider* annotation.

- The implementing class may explicitly reference a service endpoint interface through the *endpointInterface* element of the *@WebService* annotation but is not required to do so. If no *endpointInterface* is specified in *@WebService*, the service endpoint interface is implicitly defined for the implementing class.

- The business methods of the implementing class must be public and must not be declared static or final.

- The *javax.jws.WebMethod* annotation is to be used on business methods to be exposed to web service clients; if no method is annotated with *@WebMethod*, all business methods are exposed.

- Business methods that are exposed to web service clients must have JAXB-compatible parameters and return types.

- The implementing class must not be declared final and must not be abstract.

- The implementing class must have a default public constructor and must not define the finalize method.

- The implementing class may use the *javax.annotation.PostConstruct* or the *javax.annotation.PreDestroy* annotations on its methods for lifecycle event callbacks.

Requirements for building and running a JAX-WS client

A JAX-WS client can be part of any Java project and is not explicitly required to be part of a JAR/WAR archive deployed on a JavaEE container. For instance, the client might simply be contained in a quickstart Maven project as follows:

```
mvn archetype:generate -DarchetypeGroupId=org.apache.maven.archetypes -
DarchetypeArtifactId=maven-archetype-quickstart -DgroupId=com.itbuzzpress.chapter2.wsdemo -
DartifactId=client-demo-wsdl -Dversion=1.0 -Dpackage=com.itbuzzpress.chapter2.wsdemo -
Dversion=1.0 -Darchetype.interactive=false --batch-mode
```

As your client needs to reference the endpoint interface and stubs, you need to provide them either copying them from the server project or generating them again using wsconsume:

```
$ wsconsume.bat -k CustomerService.wsdl -o client-demo-wsdl\src\main\java
```

Now include a minimal Client Test application, which is part of a JUnit test case:

```
public class AppTest extends TestCase {


    public void testApp()  {
        CustomerService service = new CustomerService();
        Customer port = service.getCustomerPort();
        CustomerRecord record = port.locateCustomer("John", "Li", new USAddress());
        System.out.println("Customer record is " +record);
        assertNotNull(record);
    }
}
```

Compiling and running the test

In order to run successfully running a WS client application, a classloader needs to be properly setup to include the desired JAX-WS implementation libraries (and the required transitive dependencies, if any). Depending on the environment the client is meant to be run in, this might imply adding some jars to the classpath, or adding some artifact dependencies to the Maven dependency tree, setting the IDE properly, etc.

Since Maven is used to build the application containing the client, you can configure your *pom.xml* as follows so that it includes a dependency to the JBossWS:

```
<dependency>
    <groupId>org.jboss.ws.cxf</groupId>
    <artifactId>jbossws-cxf-client</artifactId>
    <version>4.2.3.Final</version>
    <scope>provided</scope>
</dependency>
```

Now, you can execute the testcase which will call the JAX-WS API to serve the client invocation using JBossWS.

```
mvn clean package test
```

Focus on the JAX-WS implementation used by the client

The JAX-WS implementation to be used for running a JAX-WS client is selected at runtime by looking for *META-INF/services/javax.xml.ws.spi.Provider* resources through the application classloader. Each JAX-WS implementation has a library (jar) including that resource file which internally references the proper class implementing the JAX-WS SPI Provider.

On WildFly 8.0.0.Final application server the JAX-WS implementation is contained in the *META-INF/services/javax.xml.ws.spi.Provider* of the file *jbossws-cxf-factories-4.2.3.Final*:

```
org.jboss.wsf.stack.cxf.client.ProviderImpl
```

Therefore, it is extremely important to control which artifacts or jar libraries are included in the classpath the application classloader is constructed from. If multiple implementations are found, order matters, hence the first implementation in the classpath will be used.

The safest way to avoid any classpath issue (and thus load another JAX-WS implementation) is to set the *java.endorsed.dirs* system property to include the *jbossws-cxf-factories.jar*; if you don't do that, make sure you don't include ahead of your classpath other *META-INF/services/javax.xml.ws.spi.Provider* resources which will trigger another JAX-WS implementation.

Finally, if the JAX-WS client is meant to run on WildFly as part of a JavaEE application, the JBossWS JAX-WS implementation will be automatically selected for serving the client.

Developing Web Services using WildFly

When the target container for the application being developed is known in advance, it is possible to choose among additional tools and development options provided by specific vendors.

Everything mentioned in the previous sections applies to applications meant to be deployed on WildFly 8, being it is a full JavaEE compliant container.

However, WildFly -and specifically JBossWS- provide Apache Maven plugins that greatly simplify the creation of Web Services enabled applications. In the next sections, a sample project will be created, built, deployed and tested using the WildFly tools.

Generating a basic project

Before being ready to code Web Services endpoint and clients, a project has to be properly set up in your development environment. Nowadays, the most common approach is to create a Maven project that will contain sources in standard location and allow building and testing by issuing standard commands. Maven projects can be easily imported into most IDE to prevent the user from having to manually specify where to fetch the libraries required for building and testing the project.

In the previous chapter, the *pom.xml* for a basic Maven project containing Web Services and using JBossWS has been shown. However, things get more complicated when we have both clients and server endpoints in the same project; in this case, the clients should never directly use the same classes that are used on server side in order to avoid any tight coupling between them. Hence the best approach is to generate clients automatically from the endpoint WSDL contract as part of the project build. JBossWS has Maven plugins for achieving that, but properly configuring the plugins in the *pom.xml* is a bit error prone.

To simplify this all, JBossWS offers a **Maven Archetype** to generate a sample Web Services project and deploy it easily on WildFly. The archetype can be generated from command line as follows:

```
$ mvn archetype:generate -Dfilter=org.jboss.ws.plugins.archetypes:
```

Maven will ask for the actual archetype to use, in this case we're selecting *org.jboss.ws.plugins.archetypes:jaxws-codefirst*. After that, we are required to specify the **groupId**, **artifactId** and **version** for the project being created. Finally, the Java **package** for creating the sample endpoint in can also be customized.

```
[INFO] ------------------------------------------------------------------------
```

```
[INFO] Building Maven Stub Project (No POM) 1
[INFO] ------------------------------------------------------------------------
[INFO]
[INFO] >>> maven-archetype-plugin:2.2:generate (default-cli) @ standalone-pom >>>
[INFO]
[INFO] <<< maven-archetype-plugin:2.2:generate (default-cli) @ standalone-pom <<<
[INFO]
[INFO] --- maven-archetype-plugin:2.2:generate (default-cli) @ standalone-pom ---
[INFO] Generating project in Interactive mode
[INFO] No archetype defined. Using maven-archetype-quickstart
(org.apache.maven.archetypes:maven-archetype-quickstart:1.0)
Choose archetype:
1: remote -> org.jboss.ws.plugins.archetypes:jaxws-codefirst (Creates a project for
developing a Web Service starting from Java code and using JBossWS)
Choose a number or apply filter (format: [groupId:]artifactId, case sensitive contains): :
1
Define value for property 'groupId': : com.itbuzzpress
Define value for property 'artifactId': : ws-sample
Define value for property 'version':  1.0-SNAPSHOT: :
Define value for property 'package':  com.itbuzzpress: :


[INFO] Using property: jbosswscxf = 4.2.3.Final
Confirm properties configuration:
groupId: com.itbuzzpress
artifactId: ws-sample
version: 1.0-SNAPSHOT
package: com.itbuzzpress
jbosswscxf: 4.2.3.Final


[INFO] ------------------------------------------------------------------------
[INFO] Using following parameters for creating project from Archetype: jaxws-
codefirst:1.0.0.Beta1
[INFO] ------------------------------------------------------------------------
[INFO] Parameter: groupId, Value: com.itbuzzpress
[INFO] Parameter: artifactId, Value: ws-sample
```

```
[INFO] Parameter: version, Value: 1.0-SNAPSHOT
[INFO] Parameter: package, Value: com.itbuzzpress.chapter2
[INFO] Parameter: jbosswscxf, Value: 4.2.3.Final
[INFO] ------------------------------------------------------------------------
[INFO] BUILD SUCCESS
[INFO] ------------------------------------------------------------------------
[INFO] Total time: 4:27.506s
[INFO] Finished at: Mon Feb 24 18:02:41 CET 2014
[INFO] Final Memory: 11M/205M
```

At the end of the process, the new Maven project is ready. Let's dig into the the project structure created by Maven:

```
$ tree ws-sample/
ws-sample/
|-- pom.xml
|-- README
`-- src
    |-- main
    |   `-- java
    |       `-- com
    |           `-- itbuzzpress
    |               |-- HelloWorldImpl.java
    |               |-- HelloWorld.java
    |               `-- Person.java
    `-- test
        |-- java
        |   `-- com
        |       `-- itbuzzpress
        |           |-- HelloWorldIntegrationTest.java
        |           `-- JAXWSProviderTest.java
        `-- resources
            `-- log4j.xml
```

As you can see, a sample **HelloWorld** Web Service endpoint has been created, along with a couple of testcases.The generated *pom.xml* has comments describing the most relevant sections; it includes multiple plugins for achieving different tasks:

- **maven-jaxws-tools-plugin (wsprovide)**: to generate the WSDL contract for the code-first HelloWorld endpoint (to be used to generate clients)

- **maven-jaxws-tools-plugin (wsconsume)**: to generate client stubs for the HelloWorld endpoint, to be used by the HelloWorldIntegrationTest which invokes the endpoint once it has been deployed on the server

- **maven-surefire-plugin**: with separated executions for unit and integration tests; the former is meant to run right after the compile phase, the latter are to be executed in the *integration-test* Maven phase and after the endpoint application has been deployed on the server

- **maven-war-plugin**: to package the project into a war archive

- **wildfly-maven-plugin**: to deploy the application war to a local running WildFly server

Moreover, the generated pom.xml specifies the required dependencies on the JBossWS version that's also included in WildFly 8.0.0.Final as well as proper logging and JUnit artifacts.

Importing the project in Eclipse

Once a Maven project has been created, it's time to import it in the IDE.

Assuming Eclipse is used, the process simply boils down to selecting from the upper menu **File | Import**, then choosing **Maven | Existing Maven Project**. From there click on Next and finally browsing to the file system location where the Project has been generated.

Eclipse will completely inherit the configuration from the project's *pom.xml*.

Implementing services and clients

As mentioned above, the generated project already comes with a sample Web Service endpoint:

```
@WebService(endpointInterface = "com.itbuzzpress.HelloWorld",
            targetNamespace = "http://hello.world.ns/",
            name = "HelloWorld",
            serviceName = "HelloWorldService",
            portName = "HelloWorldPort")
```

```java
@SOAPBinding(style = Style.DOCUMENT, use = Use.LITERAL)
public class HelloWorldImpl implements HelloWorld {

    public String sayHi(String text) {
        System.out.println(text);
        return "Hello " + text;
    }
    public String greetings(Person person) {
        System.out.println(person);
        return "Greetings " + person.getName() + " " + person.getSurname();
    }
}
```

HelloWorldImpl is a POJO endpoint implementing the **HelloWorld** interface, which exposes two methods with a simple (*String*) parameter and a bit more complex **Person** parameter.

The **HelloWorldImpl** endpoint full class name is referenced by the *wsprovide* plugin in the project *pom.xml*:

```xml
<plugin>
  <groupId>org.jboss.ws.plugins</groupId>
  <artifactId>maven-jaxws-tools-plugin</artifactId>
  <version>1.1.2.Final</version>
  <configuration>
    <verbose>true</verbose>
  </configuration>
  <executions>
    <execution>
      <!-- Run wsprovide to create the wsdl for the endpoint to be used later -->
      <!-- This also create the request/response wrapper classes that are also included in
the deployment (actually optional w/ JBossWS) -->
      <id>wsprovide execution</id>
      <goals>
        <goal>wsprovide</goal>
      </goals>
      <configuration>
```

```xml
      <endpointClass>com.itbuzzpress.HelloWorldImpl</endpointClass>
      <generateWsdl>true</generateWsdl>
    </configuration>
  </execution>
  <!-- ... -->
  </executions>
</plugin>
```

The plugin processes the specified endpoint class and generates the WSDL document for it, the same way the command line **wsprovide** scripts would have done. The generated contract is also the same that WildFly container will generate and expose when the endpoint will eventually be deployed.

We could modify or replace the sample endpoint with a new one, or even code additional beans. Each endpoint class we create needs a new *execution* block in the *wsprovide* plugin (each having a unique *id*) for generating the corresponding contract. We can easily clone the existing block and edit the *endpointClass* element properly.

Once we're done with the endpoint implementation, let's have a look at the client side. The sample project has an automatically generated integration testcase. Here is the *HelloWorldIntegrationTest* which is meant to be used for testing our Web Service:

```java
public class HelloWorldIntegrationTest {

    @Test
    public void testHelloWorld() throws Exception {
        HelloWorldService service = new HelloWorldService(new
URL("http://localhost:8080/ws-sample/HelloWorldService?wsdl"));
        HelloWorld port = service.getHelloWorldPort();
        Assert.assertEquals("Hello John", port.sayHi("John"));
        Person p = new Person();
        p.setName("Anne");
        p.setSurname("Li");
        Assert.assertEquals("Greetings Anne Li", port.greetings(p));
    }
}
```

HelloWorldIntegrationTest is a **JUnit integration test** meant to run against our project Web Service application after it has been deployed to the target container. The test creates a client for the endpoint included in the application deployment and invokes the operations exposed in the contract that's published for that endpoint. To achieve that, we need client stubs for the endpoint WSDL.

Usually the **wsdl-to-java** (*wsconsume*) script should be invoked to generate the required classes; those will then be manually copied into the project, imported in the IDE and used.

The sample project performs the client stub generation automatically as part of the Maven build: just before the integration test is compiled and run, the *wsconsume* plugin is run against the WSDL file that was previously generated by the *wsprovide* plugin.

```xml
<plugin>
  <groupId>org.jboss.ws.plugins</groupId>
  <artifactId>maven-jaxws-tools-plugin</artifactId>
  <version>1.1.2.Final</version>
  <configuration>
    <verbose>true</verbose>
  </configuration>
  <executions>
    <!-- ... -->
    <execution>
      <!-- Run wsconsume in generate-test-sources phase to generate the portable artifacts
for creating a test client -->
      <id>wsconsume execution</id>
      <goals>
        <goal>wsconsume-test</goal>
      </goals>
      <configuration>
        <fork>true</fork> <!-- Fork mode to specify the log conf sys prop below -->
        <argLine>-Dlog4j.output.dir=${project.build.directory}</argLine>
        <wsdls>

<wsdl>${project.build.directory}/wsprovide/resources/HelloWorldService.wsdl</wsdl>
        </wsdls>
        <targetPackage>client</targetPackage>
```

```
        <outputDirectory>${project.build.directory}/wsconsume</outputDirectory>
      </configuration>
    </execution>
  </executions>
</plugin>
```

By executing the following maven shell the plugin generates the client stubs in the package specified in *targetPackage* element; the sources for the classes are written in project's *target/generated-sources/wsconsume* directory, while the actual class files are written in project's *target/test-classes* directory.

```
mvn clean package
```

 The sources of the generated client classes can be imported too in the IDE after the first run of *wsconsume* plugin. On Eclipse that is achieved by refreshing the project, then clicking on *Project | Properties | Java Build Path | Source | Add Folder*. From there, select the *target/generated-sources/wsconsume* directory.

Should additional endpoint beans have been added before, the corresponding WSDL documents need to be referenced in additional *wsdl* blocks of the *wsprovide* plugin.

Despite having been generated against a local WSDL document, the client in *HelloWorldIntegrationTest* consumes the actually published contract at runtime (integration-test time), as the *HelloWorldService* instance is built against the remote endpoint WSDL URL.

The *HelloWorldIntegrationTest* can be extended with further tests and more integration-test classes can of course be added. The Surefire plugin in the project's *pom.xml* is configured so that any test class whose name ends with either *IntegrationTest.java* or *IntegrationTestCase.java* is run during the Maven *integration-test* phase. Any other test class is run earlier, in the *test* phase.

Deploying the Web Service application

Once both the endpoint(s) and the integration test(s) are coded, it's time to compile, package and deploy the Web Service application.

The packaging is controlled by the *maven-war-plugin*: a *ws-sample.war* archive is created, containing no *web.xml* descriptor (it's optional in Java EE6). You can use any standard tool like unzip or jar to inspect the structure of the *war* archive:

```
$ jar -tvf target/ws-sample.war
```

```
    0 wed Feb 26 23:26:20 CET 2014 META-INF/
  126 wed Feb 26 23:26:18 CET 2014 META-INF/MANIFEST.MF
    0 wed Feb 26 23:25:52 CET 2014 WEB-INF/
    0 wed Feb 26 23:25:52 CET 2014 WEB-INF/classes/
    0 wed Feb 26 23:25:52 CET 2014 WEB-INF/classes/com/
    0 wed Feb 26 23:25:52 CET 2014 WEB-INF/classes/com/itbuzzpress/
    0 wed Feb 26 23:25:52 CET 2014 WEB-INF/classes/com/itbuzzpress/jaxws/
  720 wed Feb 26 23:25:44 CET 2014 WEB-INF/classes/com/itbuzzpress/Person.class
  784 wed Feb 26 23:25:48 CET 2014 WEB-INF/classes/com/itbuzzpress/jaxws/SayHi.class
  836 wed Feb 26 23:25:48 CET 2014 WEB-
INF/classes/com/itbuzzpress/jaxws/GreetingsResponse.class
  824 wed Feb 26 23:25:48 CET 2014 WEB-
INF/classes/com/itbuzzpress/jaxws/SayHiResponse.class
  814 wed Feb 26 23:25:48 CET 2014 WEB-INF/classes/com/itbuzzpress/jaxws/Greetings.class
  354 wed Feb 26 23:25:44 CET 2014 WEB-INF/classes/com/itbuzzpress/HelloWorld.class
 1709 wed Feb 26 23:25:44 CET 2014 WEB-INF/classes/com/itbuzzpress/HelloWorldImpl.class
 8089 Mon Feb 24 18:02:42 CET 2014 META-INF/maven/com.itbuzzpress/ws-sample/pom.xml
  116 wed Feb 26 23:26:18 CET 2014 META-INF/maven/com.itbuzzpress/ws-sample/pom.properties
```

Of course, the *HelloWorld* interface and its implementation class are included. Few classes in *com.itbuzzpress.jaxws* package are also included: they are the JAXB annotated class artifacts generated by *wsprovide* plugin. Actually, WildFly could also process a deployment without them, but they make the deployment portable. The sources for those classes are available in project's *target/wsprovide/java* directory.

The sample project *pom.xml* comes with the *wildfly-maven-plugin*, so triggering the deployment against a locally running WildFly instance is straightforward:

```
$ mvn wildfly:deploy
```

The build will go through the compile, test and package phases and eventually connect to the application server to deploy the application. The server log will show something like this to confirm the deployment was successful:

```
00:42:55,689 INFO  [org.jboss.as.repository] (management-handler-thread - 1) JBAS014900:
Content added at location /dati/wildfly-
8.0.0.Final/standalone/data/content/b9/2ed09f453cc1f9209a17c72144f69d3a674ddd/content
00:42:55,711 INFO  [org.jboss.as.server.deployment] (MSC service thread 1-5) JBAS015876:
Starting deployment of "ws-sample.war" (runtime-name: "ws-sample.war")
```

```
00:42:55,934 INFO  [org.jboss.ws.cxf.metadata] (MSC service thread 1-4) JBWS024061: Adding
service endpoint metadata: id=com.itbuzzpress.HelloWorldImpl

 address=http://localhost:8080/ws-sample/HelloWorldService

 implementor=com.itbuzzpress.HelloWorldImpl

 serviceName={http://hello.world.ns/}HelloWorldService

 portName={http://hello.world.ns/}HelloWorldPort

 annotationWsdlLocation=null

 wsdlLocationOverride=null

 mtomEnabled=false

00:42:56,088 INFO  [org.apache.cxf.service.factory.ReflectionServiceFactoryBean] (MSC
service thread 1-4) Creating Service {http://hello.world.ns/}HelloWorldService from class
com.itbuzzpress.HelloWorld

00:42:56,372 INFO  [org.apache.cxf.endpoint.ServerImpl] (MSC service thread 1-4) Setting
the server's publish address to be http://localhost:8080/ws-sample/HelloWorldService

00:42:56,424 INFO  [org.jboss.ws.cxf.deployment] (MSC service thread 1-4) JBWS024074: WSDL
published to: file:/dati/wildfly-8.0.0.Final/standalone/data/wsdl/ws-
sample.war/HelloWorldService.wsdl

00:42:56,440 INFO  [org.jboss.as.webservices] (MSC service thread 1-6) JBAS015539: Starting
service jboss.ws.endpoint."ws-sample.war"."com.itbuzzpress.HelloWorldImpl"

00:42:56,524 INFO  [org.wildfly.extension.undertow] (MSC service thread 1-4) JBAS017534:
Registered web context: /ws-sample

00:42:56,640 INFO  [org.jboss.as.server] (management-handler-thread - 1) JBAS018559:
Deployed "ws-sample.war" (runtime-name : "ws-sample.war")
```

From the Administration console of WildFly, you can check that the Web Service endpoint has been actually published. You can reach the following UI by selecting the **Runtime** upper tab and then choosing from the left side menu: **Subsystems | Webservices**:

WEBSERVICES

▲ Name	Context	Deployment
com.itbuzzpress.chapter2.HelloWorldImpl	ws-sample	ws-sample.war

Name:	com.itbuzzpress.chapter2.HelloWorldImpl
Context:	ws-sample
Class:	com.itbuzzpress.chapter2.HelloWorldImpl
Type:	JAXWS_JSE
WSDL Url:	http://localhost:8080/ws-sample/HelloWorldService?wsdl
Deployment:	ws-sample.war

Later, after having tested the application, a similar command can be used to undeploy and remove the application from the application server:

```
$ mvn wildfly:undeploy
```

Running the testsuite

The unit tests should have been already executed when compiling and deploying the application, given they live in an early phase of the build.

The integration tests, instead, are meant to run after the install phase and hence need to be explicitly triggered, after the application has been properly deployed (as a matter of fact, the integration test usually call in when services are available on the target container):

```
$ mvn integration-test
```

The *HelloWorldIntegrationTest* is run and that performs the actual Web Service calls to the HelloWorld endpoint from the sample application.

Next steps

Now that you've successfully tried the sample, you can start hacking on it. Apart from modifying the endpoint and/or adding new ones, you might want to use the sample *pom.xml* as a starting point for more complex scenarios; for instance, you could:

- Start with contract first endpoints; a *wsconsume* plugin run can be added specifying *wsconsume* in the *goal* element and processing a local or remove WSDL document. The manually coded endpoint implementation will have to implement the generated endpoint interface

- Have Web Service clients in the actual application deployment archive: similarly, to the previous point, a *wsconsume* plugin run could be used to generate the stubs automatically.

Chapter 3: Advanced JAX-WS and JAXB usage

This chapter covers some advanced concepts that are often required to deal with non-trivial web services applications. Those include:

- Oneway invocations

- JAX-WS handlers

- JavaEE injection and JAX-WS components

- Asynchronous invocations

- Fault handling

Finally, this chapter will cover some examples of explicit use of JAXB annotations to deal with complex type exchanges in SOAP messages.

Oneway invocations

Most of the message-exchange-patterns are request-response ones; however in some scenarios oneway invocations are preferred, as the client does not expect any actual data in the response from the server. In such cases, the server is instructed that no SOAP response message has to be sent back to the client, whose low-level invocation is immediately acknowledged (for instance with a HTTP 202 response code if the HTTP transport is in use). Moreover the endpoint processing can be (and usually is) performed in a separate thread, freeing resources that can be used to promptly serve other requests.

Oneway operations in WSDL documents simply have no {http://schemas.xmlsoap.org/wsdl/}output elements. On Java code, the @javax.jws.Oneway annotation is used as follows:

```
@WebService
public class MyServiceEndpoint {
    @Oneway
    public void ping() {
        //...
    }
}
```

JAX-WS Handlers

The JAX-WS specification defines a flexible plugin framework for message processing components (handlers) that can be used to extend or customize the capabilities of a JAX-WS application.

Handlers can be provided with a JAX-WS application and attached to client proxies and server endpoints, which are known as binding providers. Both client and server-side handlers are organized into ordered lists known as a **handler chains**. The handlers within a handler chain are invoked each time a message is sent or received. **Inbound** messages are processed by handlers prior to binding provider processing. **Outbound** messages are processed by handlers after any binding provider processing.

Handlers are invoked with a message context that provides methods to access and modify inbound and outbound messages and to manage a set of properties. Message context properties may be used to facilitate communication between individual handlers and between handlers, clients and service endpoints. Different types of handlers are invoked with different types of message context.

The following picture depicts the two types of handlers which are available, that is **Logical** Handlers and **Protocol** handlers (also known as SOAP Handlers) which are detailed in the next section:

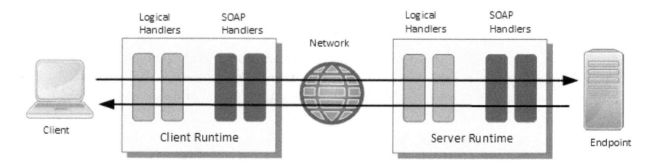

Logical Handlers

Logical Handlers only operate on message context properties and message payloads; they are protocol agnostic and are unable to affect protocol specific parts of a message. Logical handlers are handlers implementing the *javax.xml.ws.handler.LogicalHandler* interface and being passed *javax.xml.ws.handler.LogicalMessageContext* instances. Here is an example:

```java
public class SampleLogicalHandler implements LogicalHandler<LogicalMessageContext> {
    @Override
    public boolean handleMessage(LogicalMessageContext context) {
        //...
        return true;
    }
    @Override
    public boolean handleFault(LogicalMessageContext context) {
        //...
        return true;
    }
    @Override
    public void close(MessageContext context) {
        //...
    }
}
```

Any JAX-WS handler implementation must implement the **handleMessage** and **handleFault** and **close** methods.

The *handleMessage* method is invoked by the JAX-WS runtime for normal message processing; *handlerFault* method is invoked for fault message processing instead. Both methods return a boolean value, that can be used by the handler implementer to control the processing flow in the handler chain.

- If *true* is returned, the processing goes on with the next handler of the chain; the next handler's *handleMessage* or *handleFault* method will be invoked, depending on the current method being a *handleMessage* or *handleFault*.

- If *false* is returned, the message processing is meant to cease. In the case of *handleFault* method, the runtime will invoke *close* on each previously invoked handler in the chain and eventually dispatch the fault message. In the case of *handleMessage* method, instead, the behavior depends on the message-exchange-pattern (MEP) being request-response or not.

o   For **request-response MEP**, the handler chain processing direction is reversed, the request message becomes a response message and the runtime invokes *handleMessage* methods on the next handlers (which are the previously invoked ones, due to the direction change), until the message is eventually dispatched.

o   For **oneway MEP**, instead, normal message processing stops, *close* is called on each previously invoked handler in the chain and the message is eventually dispatched.

In any case, the *close* method is called for each handler at the end of the message-exchange-pattern, just before the final message / fault dispatching; it allows users to clean-up resources that might have been allocated in the handlers.

Protocol Handlers

Protocol Handlers operate on message context properties and protocol specific messages. Protocol handlers are specific to a particular protocol and may access and change protocol specific aspects of a message. They implement any interface derived from *javax.xml.ws.handler.Handler* except *javax.xml.ws.handler.LogicalHandler*. Below is an example of a **SOAP protocol handler**:

```java
public class SampleSOAPHandler implements SOAPHandler<SOAPMessageContext>{
    @Override
    public boolean handleMessage(SOAPMessageContext context) { //...
        return true;
    }
    @Override
    public boolean handleFault(SOAPMessageContext context) {  //...
        return true;
    }
    @Override
    public void close(MessageContext context) {    //... }

    @Override
    public Set<QName> getHeaders() { //...
        return null;
    }
}
```

As you can see, the above Handler implements *javax.xml.ws.handler.soap.SOAPHandler* interface and receives in its *handleMessage* and *handleFault* methods the *javax.xml.ws.handler.soap.SOAPMessageContext* instances.

On the other hand, the *getHeaders* method from *SOAPHandler* interface has to be implemented and is expected to return the SOAP message header blocks that can be processed by this handler.

The mechanism for processing handlers in the chain and eventually reaching message dispatch is the same described in the previous section for logical handlers.

The Message Context interface

As mentioned above, different implementations of *javax.xml.ws.handler.MessageContext* interface will be passed to user handlers, depending on the actual handler type. In fact, *MessageContext* is the super interface for all JAX-WS message contexts. It extends *Map<String,Object>* with additional methods and constants to manage a set of properties that enable handlers in a handler chain to share processing related state. For example, a handler may use the *put* method to insert a property in the message context that one or more other handlers in the handler chain may subsequently obtain via the *get* method.

Properties are scoped as either HANDLER or APPLICATION. Properties in the former scope are only available to the handlers of the chain, while those in the latter scope are also made available to client applications and service endpoint implementations. The default scope for a property is HANDLER.

- **Logical handlers** are passed *LogicalMessageContext* instances, which provide a *getMessage* method giving access to the payload (only) of the message being processed.

- **SOAP handlers**, instead, are passed instances of *SOAPMessageContext* interface, which extends the base *MessageContext* with methods giving access and allowing changes to the full message being processed, including headers.

Configuring client and endpoint handlers

Handlers are configured and attached to client proxies programmatically using the JAX-WS API. On server side, handlers are bound to endpoints using deployment metadata, usually through the JSR-181 **@javax.jws.HandlerChain** annotation. In the following section, we will see how to configure handlers both on the Client side and on the server side.

Client side

On client side, the proxy is casted to *BindingProvider* to get the handler chain, modify it and set it back:

```java
import javax.xml.ws.BindingProvider;
import javax.xml.ws.handler.Handler;
//...
Service service = Service.create(wsdlURL, serviceName);
Endpoint port = (Endpoint)service.getPort(Endpoint.class);
BindingProvider bindingProvider = (BindingProvider)port;


List<Handler> handlerChain = new ArrayList<Handler>();
handlerChain.add(new SampleSOAPHandler());
handlerChain.add(new SampleLogicalHandler());
bindingProvider.getBinding().setHandlerChain(handlerChain); // important!
```

Server side

On server side, the *@HandlerChain* annotation is used to reference a descriptor listing the handlers to be configured for the given endpoint:

```java
import javax.jws.HandlerChain;
//...
@WebService
@HandlerChain(file = "jaxws-server-handlers.xml")
public class MySOAPEndpointImpl {

    //...
}
```

The location of the handler file can be:

- An absolute URL in external form (for example http://www.foo.com/bar/handlers.xml)

- A relative path from the current class file

The JAX-WS specification describes the exact format of the file descriptor; below is an example of the file *jaxws-server-handlers.xml*, which defines two handlers: a Logical Handler named **SampleLogicalHandler** and a SOAP Handler named **SampleSOAPHandler**:

```xml
<?xml version="1.0" encoding="UTF-8"?>
<handler-chains xmlns="http://java.sun.com/xml/ns/javaee"
                xmlns:xsi="http://www.w3.org/2001/XMLSchema-instance"
                xsi:schemaLocation="http://java.sun.com/xml/ns/javaee
javaee_web_services_1_2.xsd">
   <handler-chain>
      <protocol-bindings>##SOAP11_HTTP ##SOAP12_HTTP</protocol-bindings>
      <handler>
         <handler-name>SampleLogicalHandler</handler-name>
         <handler-class>com.itbuzzpress.chapter3.handler.SampleLogicalHandler</handler-class>
      </handler>
      <handler>
         <handler-name>SampleSOAPHandler</handler-name>
         <handler-class>com.itbuzzpress.chapter3.handler.SampleSOAPHandler</handler-class>
      </handler>
   </handler-chain>
</handler-chains>
```

Handler chains are defined for a given protocol binding (for instance SOAP 1.1, SOAP 1.2). Handlers are identified by the name and full-qualified classname.

 The descriptor-based approach can be used as well for handlers attached to Web Service clients; the Service Endpoint Interface used by the client proxy has to be annotated with *@HandlerChain*.

JavaEE injection and JAX-WS components

Most of the JavaEE components can be automatically injected in user classes by the container, for instance through the resource pattern exemplified by the *javax.annotation.Resource* annotation in JSR-250.

When a Web Services application is running in a JavaEE environment, it can leverage the various EE injection mechanisms in JAX-WS components (endpoints, handlers) and allows to easily setup JAX-WS client references.

@WebServiceRef

The *javax.xml.wsWebServiceRef* annotation is used to define a reference to a web service and (optionally) an injection target for it. It can be used to inject both Web Service clients and proxy instances. Web Service references are resources in the JavaEE sense and can be injected in JavaEE components, including servlets, EJB3 beans and CDI beans. Here is an example:

```
import java.io.IOException;
import javax.servlet.ServletException;
import javax.servlet.http.HttpServlet;
import javax.servlet.http.HttpServletRequest;
import javax.servlet.http.HttpServletResponse;
import javax.xml.ws.WebServiceRef;

public class MyServletClient extends HttpServlet {
    @WebServiceRef(value = MyService.class, wsdlLocation = "WEB-INF/wsdl/MyService.wsdl")
    public MyService service;
    @WebServiceRef(value = MyService.class)
    public MyEndpoint port;


    @Override
    protected void doGet(HttpServletRequest req, HttpServletResponse res) throws
ServletException, IOException {
        res.getWriter().write(port.echo("foo"));
    }
}
```

The *service* and *port* fields of the Servlet are injected references to the *MyService* Web Service client and the *MyEndpoint* corresponding port proxy. Just to clarify, here is how the *MyService* class would look like:

```
import java.net.URL;
import javax.xml.namespace.QName;
import javax.xml.ws.Service;
import javax.xml.ws.WebEndpoint;
import javax.xml.ws.WebServiceClient;
```

```
import javax.xml.ws.WebServiceFeature;


@WebServiceClient(name = "ServiceOne", targetNamespace = "http://itbuzzpress.com/test",
wsdlLocation = "WEB-INF/wsdl/MyService.wsdl")
public class MyService extends Service {
    public MyService(URL wsdlLocation, QName serviceName) {
        super(wsdlLocation, serviceName);
    }
    @WebEndpoint(name = "MyEndpoint")
    public MyEndpoint getMyEndpointPort() {
        return super.getPort(new QName("http://itbuzzpress.com/test", "MyEndpointPort"),
MyEndpoint.class);
    }
    @WebEndpoint(name = "MyEndpoint")
    public MyEndpoint getMyEndpointPort(WebServiceFeature... features) {
        return super.getPort(new QName("http://itbuzzpress.com/test", "MyEndpointPort"),
MyEndpoint.class, features);
    }
}
```

In order to resolve the WSDL contract for the referenced service, the JAX-WS runtime will use the *wsdlLocation* attribute specified in the *@WebServiceClient* annotation in the service class. The *wsdlLocation* attribute in the *@WebServiceRef* annotation can be used to override the value. This is convenient for example, when we need the client to be created against an equivalent WSDL contract stored in a different location from the one the service class has been generated from.

 The *wsdlLocation*, as well as the other optional attributes of *javax.xml.wsWebServiceRef* annotation, can also be specified using deployment descriptors supported by the JavaEE container in use. Moreover, if no *wsdlLocation* is specified at all, the container is expected to resolve the reference by matching the service QName with those of the endpoints currently deployed on the same container the reference is being processed on.

@Resource

The *@javax.annotation.Resource* annotation can be used in JAX-WS endpoint and handler classes for container injection, as described in JSR-250.

A notable use case, though, is the resource injection of *javax.xml.ws.WebServiceContext* references in JAX-WS endpoint implementations. The *WebServiceContext* can be used for instance for retrieving the current *MessageContext* instance, which is the same object accessed by properly configured handlers for the endpoint. So for instance, the endpoint can access and modify information read / written by handlers.

In the following example, the context is used to figure out the scheme (*http*, *https*) used when sending the SOAP message that triggered the current WS invocation served by the endpoint

```
import javax.annotation.Resource;
import javax.jws.WebService;
import javax.servlet.http.HttpServletRequest;
import javax.xml.ws.WebServiceContext;
import javax.xml.ws.handler.MessageContext;

@WebService(...)
public class MyServiceEndpoint {
    @Resource
    private WebServiceContext webServiceCtx;

    public String sayHi(String arg) {
        MessageContext ctx = webServiceCtx.getMessageContext();
        HttpServletRequest hsr = (HttpServletRequest)ctx.get(MessageContext.SERVLET_REQUEST);
        String scheme = hsr.getScheme();
        return "Hi";
    }
}
```

Asynchronous invocations

When dealing with service operations requiring complex (and hence long lasting) computations, it might be convenient for the client to avoid a synchronous waiting for the server response message. For such scenarios, JAX-WS offers two asynchronous approaches, based on **polling** and **callbacks**.

Let's take as starting point the following endpoint definition:

```
@WebService(...)
public interface MyServiceEndpoint {
    @WebMethod
    public String echo(@WebParam(name = "String_1") String string1);
}
```

On client side, the user is expected to enrich it by adding interface methods with -*Async* suffix. The first (polling approach) returns a *javax.xml.ws.Response* holder of the original response type @WebMethod(operationName = "echo"):

```
public javax.xml.ws.Response<String> echoAsync(@WebParam(name = "String_1") String
string1);
```

The second (callback approach) returns a *java.util.concurrent.Future* instance and accepts an additional *javax.xml.ws.AsynchHandler* object as parameter.

```
@WebMethod(operationName = "echo")
public java.util.concurrent.Future<?> echoAsync(@WebParam(name = "String_1") String
string1, @WebParam(name = "asyncHandler") javax.xml.ws.AsyncHandler<String> asyncHandler);
```

The two methods can be used in the client code to avoid waiting on the response from the server. The *Response* class has a *isDone* method that allows checking if the response has actually been received before eventually calling the *get* method to retrieve it.

```
Response<String> resp = port.echoAsync("Foo");
while(!resp.isDone()) {
    //do something
}
resp.get();
```

The callback approach can be used by first defining a class that implements the *AsynchHandler* interface and then passing it to the proxy:

```
AsyncHandler<String> handler = new AsyncHandler<String>() {
    @Override
    public void handleResponse(Response<String> response) {
        String retStr = response.get();
        //...
    }
};
Future<?> future = port.echoAsync("Hello", handler);
```

Of course, the handler will be called in a different thread when the response message is received.

JAXB binding and complex types

As explained in the first chapter, the **JAXB** specification defines how XML schemas included in the WSDL contract are to be mapped to Java classes and hence how SOAP messages conforming to the contract are to be converted into instances of such classes. The available JAXB implementation is automatically leveraged by the JAX-WS stack in use.

As JAXB comes with sensible defaults, users don't usually need to explicitly care about its annotations or spend time looking at the matching details between the contract and the Java model. This is especially true when there are no specific requirements on generated WSDL contracts for code-first developed endpoints and when the generated Java model from an existing contract is acceptable.

That being said, there are still scenarios requiring users to customize the binding between the schema and the Java model, for instance to control how Java collections are converted into XML, or how String from XML messages are parsed into Java numbers, etc.

The following paragraphs provide some notable customization examples; users should still have a look at the JAXB specification (https://jcp.org/aboutJava/communityprocess/mrel/jsr222/index2.html) for a thorough description of all the available JAXB annotation and the default mappings available.

 As a general suggestion, the Java-to-WSDL and WSDL-to-Java tools are very convenient solutions for getting a decent binding quickly; once your Java model is mapped to a contract, it's usually quite simple to apply slight changes (for instance adding, removing or tuning annotations) to achieve the desired final mapping.

Treating a field as an XML attribute or element

When mapping a Java bean to schema type, by default each class field is converted to an *element* of the *sequence* the *complexType* is composed of. Consider the following simple SampleBean POJO class:

```
public class SampleBean {
       private String firstField;
       private String secondField;

       public String getFirstField() {
             return firstField;
       }
       public void setFirstField(String firstField) {
             this.firstField = firstField;
       }
       public String getSecondField() {
             return secondField;
       }
       public void setSecondField(String secondField) {
             this.secondField = secondField;
       }
}
```

The above Java Bean would be mapped to a schema like that, where each field of the class is bound to an element (the actual namespaces depends are derived from the class package, etc.):

```
<xs:complexType name="sampleBean">
  <xs:sequence>
    <xs:element minOccurs="0" name="firstField" type="xs:string"/>
    <xs:element minOccurs="0" name="secondField" type="xs:string"/>
  </xs:sequence>
</xs:complexType>
```

In some cases, though, it might be required to bind a field of the class to an **attribute** instead of an element. To achieve that, JAXB offers the *@javax.xml.bind.annotation.XmlAttribute* annotation, which can be added to the Java bean getter method for the corresponding field.

61

The *@XmlAttribute* usage is demonstrated in the *field-binding-sample* project, which is created using the *jaxws-codefirst* Maven archetype introduced before. As you can see, the *HelloWorld* endpoint has been replaced by the following *SampleEndpoint* class:

```java
@WebService(targetNamespace = "http://field.binding.ns/",
                name = "SampleEndpoint",
                serviceName = "SampleEndpointService",
                portName = "SampleEndpointPort")
public class SampleEndpoint {
    @WebMethod
    public SampleBean echo(SampleBean bean) {
        System.out.println("process: " + bean);
        return bean;
    }
}
```

The *SampleBean* class used as parameter and result of the endpoint operation is defined as follows:

```java
public class SampleBean {
    private String firstField;
    private String secondField;
    @XmlAttribute
    public String getFirstField() {
        return firstField;
    }
    public void setFirstField(String firstField) {
        this.firstField = firstField;
    }
    public String getSecondField() {
        return secondField;
    }
    public void setSecondField(String secondField) {
        this.secondField = secondField;
    }
}
```

Note the **@XmlAttribute** annotation on the *getFirstField()* method. Finally, the project *pom.xml* is modified to reference *com.itbuzzpress.SampleEndpoint* as *endpointClass* in the wsprovide execution and to reference *SampleEndpointService.wsdl* as *wsdl* in the wsconsume execution.

The project can eventually be built and the endpoint application deployed to WildFly, through the usual *mvn wildfly:deploy* command. A simple client integration test is coded as below, using the classes generated by wsconsume:

```
import java.net.URL;
import org.junit.*;
import client.*;


public class SampleEndpointIntegrationTest {
    @Test
    public void testSampleEndpoint() throws Exception {
        SampleEndpointService service = new SampleEndpointService(new
URL("http://localhost:8080/field-binding-sample/SampleEndpointService?wsdl"));
        SampleEndpoint port = service.getSampleEndpointPort();
        SampleBean bean = new SampleBean();
        bean.setFirstField("Foo");
        bean.setSecondField("Bar");
        SampleBean result = port.echo(bean);
        Assert.assertEquals("Foo", result.getFirstField());
        Assert.assertEquals("Bar", result.getSecondField());
    }
}
```

Running the testsuite (using *mvn integration-test*) proves proper marshalling and unmarshalling of Java objects is performed, as the following type is defined in the generated and published WSDL:

```
<xs:complexType name="sampleBean">
  <xs:sequence>
    <xs:element minOccurs="0" name="secondField" type="xs:string"/>
  </xs:sequence>
  <xs:attribute name="firstField" type="xs:string"/>
</xs:complexType>
```

Here follows the SOAP request, which goes over the wire containing the firstField and secondField from the SampleBean class:

```
<soap:Envelope xmlns:soap="http://schemas.xmlsoap.org/soap/envelope/">
  <soap:Body>
    <ns2:echo xmlns:ns2="http://field.binding.ns/">
      <arg0 firstField="Foo">
        <secondField>Bar</secondField>
      </arg0>
    </ns2:echo>
  </soap:Body>
</soap:Envelope>
```

And here is the corresponding response:

```
<soap:Envelope xmlns:soap="http://schemas.xmlsoap.org/soap/envelope/">
  <soap:Body>
    <ns2:echoResponse xmlns:ns2="http://field.binding.ns/">
      <return firstField="Foo">
        <secondField>Bar</secondField>
      </return>
    </ns2:echoResponse>
  </soap:Body>
</soap:Envelope>
```

As you can see, *firstField* is treated as an XML attribute, while *secondField* is treated as an XML element.

List Bindings

By default, Java *List* maps to a *complexType* in XML schemas; that type contains a *sequence* of a single *element* with *maxOccurs="unbounded"*. For simple lists, this might be conveniently replaced by a {http://www.w3.org/2001/XMLSchema}*list* relying on the JAXB *@javax.xml.bind.annotation.XmlList* annotation.

The *@XmlList* usage is demonstrated in the *list-binding-sample* project. The project (available on github at: https://github.com/asoldano/jaxws-book/tree/master/chapter3/list-binding-sample) has been created using the *jaxws-codefirst* Maven archetype introduced before.

64

Here is the new endpoint class that we will use:

```
@WebService(targetNamespace = "http://list.binding.ns/",
                name = "SampleEndpoint",
                serviceName = "SampleEndpointService",
                portName = "SampleEndpointPort")


public class SampleEndpoint {

    @WebMethod
    public List<String> process(List<String> list) {
            System.out.println("process: " + list);
            return list;
    }


    @WebMethod
    @XmlList
    public List<String> processXmlList(@XmlList List<String> list) {
            System.out.println("processXmlList: " + list);
            return list;
    }
}
```

Two methods with the same signature and implementation are included, but different name and annotations are defined.

 The *processXmlList* method is annotated twice with **@XmlList** to tell the container that both the return and parameter lists are to be bound to simple *xs:list*.

Finally, the project *pom.xml* is modified to reference **com.itbuzzpress.SampleEndpoint** as *endpointClass* in the wsprovide execution and to reference **SampleEndpointService.wsdl** as *wsdl* in the wsconsume execution.

The project can eventually be built and the endpoint application deployed to WildFly, through the usual *mvn wildfly:deploy* command. A simple client integration test is coded as below, using the classes generated by *wsconsume*:

```
import java.net.URL;
import java.util.LinkedList;
import java.util.List;
import org.junit.Assert;
import org.junit.Test;
import client.SampleEndpoint;
import client.SampleEndpointService;

public class SampleEndpointIntegrationTest {

    @Test
    public void testSampleEndpoint() throws Exception {
        SampleEndpointService service = new SampleEndpointService(new
URL("http://localhost:8080/list-binding-sample/SampleEndpointService?wsdl"));
        SampleEndpoint port = service.getSampleEndpointPort();
        List<String> list = new LinkedList<String>();
        list.add("Foo");
        list.add("Bar");
        List<String> processResult = port.process(list);
        Assert.assertEquals(2, processResult.size());
        Assert.assertTrue(processResult.contains("Foo"));
        Assert.assertTrue(processResult.contains("Bar"));
        List<String> processXmlListResult = port.processXmlList(list);
        Assert.assertEquals(2, processXmlListResult.size());
        Assert.assertTrue(processXmlListResult.contains("Foo"));
        Assert.assertTrue(processXmlListResult.contains("Bar"));
    }
}
```

Running the testsuite (using as usual *mvn integration-test* command) shows the different binding of lists for the two endpoint operations.

As expected, the generated WSDL contract includes different *complexType* blocks for the request and response messages corresponding to the *process* and *processXmlList* operations.

Here follows an excerpt of the WSDL that shows how the two different operations have been coded:

```
<xs:complexType name="processXmlList">
  <xs:sequence>
    <xs:element minOccurs="0" name="arg0">
      <xs:simpleType>
        <xs:list itemType="xs:string"/>
      </xs:simpleType>
    </xs:element>
  </xs:sequence>
</xs:complexType>
<xs:complexType name="processXmlListResponse">
  <xs:sequence>
    <xs:element minOccurs="0" name="return">
      <xs:simpleType>
        <xs:list itemType="xs:string"/>
      </xs:simpleType>
    </xs:element>
  </xs:sequence>
</xs:complexType>

<xs:complexType name="process">
  <xs:sequence>
    <xs:element maxOccurs="unbounded" minOccurs="0" name="arg0" type="xs:string"/>
  </xs:sequence>
</xs:complexType>
<xs:complexType name="processResponse">
  <xs:sequence>
    <xs:element maxOccurs="unbounded" minOccurs="0" name="return" type="xs:string"/>
  </xs:sequence>
</xs:complexType>
```

Now let's see the SOAP messages which are going on the wire. At first, we will show the **process** request:

```
<soap:Envelope xmlns:soap="http://schemas.xmlsoap.org/soap/envelope/">
  <soap:Body>
    <ns2:process xmlns:ns2="http://list.binding.ns/">
      <arg0>Foo</arg0>
      <arg0>Bar</arg0>
    </ns2:process>
  </soap:Body>
</soap:Envelope>
```

This is the corresponding **processResponse**:

```
<soap:Envelope xmlns:soap="http://schemas.xmlsoap.org/soap/envelope/">
  <soap:Body>
    <ns2:processResponse xmlns:ns2="http://list.binding.ns/">
      <return>Foo</return>
      <return>Bar</return>
    </ns2:processResponse>
  </soap:Body>
</soap:Envelope>
```

As you can see, when invoking the **processXMLList** method, the arguments are more compact:

```
<soap:Envelope xmlns:soap="http://schemas.xmlsoap.org/soap/envelope/">
  <soap:Body>
    <ns2:processXmlList xmlns:ns2="http://list.binding.ns/">
      <arg0>Foo Bar</arg0>
    </ns2:processXmlList>
  </soap:Body>
</soap:Envelope>
```

And here is the corresponding **processXMLListResponse**:

```
<soap:Envelope xmlns:soap="http://schemas.xmlsoap.org/soap/envelope/">
  <soap:Body>
    <ns2:processXmlListResponse xmlns:ns2="http://list.binding.ns/">
```

```
          <return>Foo Bar</return>
      </ns2:processXmlListResponse>
    </soap:Body>
</soap:Envelope>
```

When dealing with huge lists, the usage of list bindings makes a big difference in terms of final payload message size, as less bytes are spent on return element tags.

Adapters and custom bindings

One the most powerful customization mechanisms offered by **JAXB** is the *javax.xml.bind.annotation.adapters.XmlAdapter* class.

```
public abstract class XmlAdapter<ValueType,BoundType> {

    ...

    public abstract BoundType unmarshal(ValueType v) throws Exception;
    public abstract ValueType marshal(BoundType v) throws Exception;
}
```

Users can provide custom classes extending *XmlAdapter* to control how value types (usually strings in the XML message) are converted to and from bound types (classes in the Java model). This can be very useful in the following use cases:

- When dealing with edge cases that would otherwise result in errors (like unmarshalling a *XMLGregorianCalendar* from an empty string)

- When binding XML types to Java types different from the default ones

- If you are going to unmarshal XML types in a custom way

 The *XmlAdapter* classes are referenced using the JAXB *@javax.xml.bind.annotation.adapters.XmlJavaTypeAdapter* annotation.

The *@XmlJavaTypeAdapter* usage is demonstrated in the *custom-binding-sample* project (hosted at https://github.com/asoldano/jaxws-book/tree/master/chapter3/custom-binding-sample). As usual, this project has been created using the *jaxws-codefirst* Maven archetype introduced before.

The following endpoint class is included in the project:

```java
import javax.jws.WebMethod;
import javax.jws.WebService;
import javax.xml.bind.annotation.adapters.XmlJavaTypeAdapter;


@WebService(targetNamespace = "http://custom.binding.ns/",
                name = "SampleEndpoint",
                serviceName = "SampleEndpointService",
                portName = "SampleEndpointPort")


public class SampleEndpoint {
      @WebMethod
      public String process(String s) {
             System.out.println("process: " + s);
             return s;
      }


      @WebMethod
      @XmlJavaTypeAdapter(SampleAdapter.class)
      public SampleBean processCustom(@XmlJavaTypeAdapter(SampleAdapter.class) SampleBean
bean) {
             System.out.println("processCustom: fistAttribute=" + bean.getFistAttribute() +
", secondAttribute=" + bean.getSecondAttribute());
             return bean;
      }
}
```

Two methods are provided; the first one (*process*) is a simple string echo, while the second (*processCustom*) merely dumps the *SampleBean* instance. Two **@XmlJavaTypeAdapter** annotations tell the container that the *SampleAdapter* class is to be used for both the return and parameter objects. Here is the **SampleBean** class, which is a basic POJO containing the fields *firstAttribute* and *secondAttribute*:

```java
public class SampleBean {
      private String firstAttribute;
      private Long secondAttribute;
```

```
        public String getFirstAttribute() {
              return fistAttribute;
        }
        public void setFirstAttribute(String firstAttribute) {
              this.firstAttribute = firstAttribute;
        }
        public Long getSecondAttribute() {
              return secondAttribute;
        }
        public void setSecondAttribute(Long secondAttribute) {
              this.secondAttribute = secondAttribute;
        }
}
```

The *SampleAdapter* class, on the other hand, is an extension of *XmlAdapter* performing a custom tokenization and conversion of a String into the fields of a *SampleBean*:

```
import javax.xml.bind.annotation.adapters.XmlAdapter;

public class SampleAdapter extends XmlAdapter<String, SampleBean> {
      @Override
      public String marshal(SampleBean v) throws Exception {
            return v.getFistAttribute() + "-" + v.getSecondAttribute();
      }
      @Override
      public SampleBean unmarshal(String v) throws Exception {
            SampleBean b = new SampleBean();
            b.setFistAttribute(v.substring(0, v.indexOf('-')));
            b.setSecondAttribute(Long.valueOf(v.substring(v.indexOf('-') + 1)));
            return b;
      }
}
```

Finally, the project *pom.xml* is modified to reference **com.itbuzzpress.SampleEndpoint** as *endpointClass* in the wsprovide execution and to reference **SampleEndpointService.wsdl** as *wsdl* in the wsconsume execution.

As usual, the project can eventually be built and the endpoint application deployed to WildFly, through the usual *mvn wildfly:deploy* command.

A simple client integration test is coded as below, using the classes generated by *wsconsume*:

```
package com.itbuzzpress;


import java.net.URL;
import org.junit.Assert;
import org.junit.Test;
import client.SampleEndpoint;
import client.SampleEndpointService;


public class SampleEndpointIntegrationTest {

    @Test
    public void testSampleEndpoint() throws Exception {
        SampleEndpointService service = new SampleEndpointService(new
URL("http://localhost:8080/custom-binding-sample/SampleEndpointService?wsdl"));
        SampleEndpoint port = service.getSampleEndpointPort();
        Assert.assertEquals("Foo-45", port.process("Foo-45"));
        Assert.assertEquals("Bar-34", port.processCustom("Bar-34"));
    }
}
```

As can be inferred by the above code, on client side the two operation methods of the generated port have the same signature. They both accept and return a String. That's because on server side *processCustom* method, we declared the adapter binding our SampleBean class to a String.

As a consequence, the WSDL contract generated by *wsprovide* and consumed by *wsconsume* to create the client stub uses Strings for both operations request parameters and responses.

For the sake of completeness, we will include here the *SampleEndpoint* generated client endpoint interface:

```java
package client;

import javax.jws.WebMethod;
import javax.jws.WebParam;
import javax.jws.WebResult;
import javax.jws.WebService;
import javax.xml.bind.annotation.XmlSeeAlso;
import javax.xml.ws.RequestWrapper;
import javax.xml.ws.ResponseWrapper;


@WebService(targetNamespace = "http://custom.binding.ns/", name = "SampleEndpoint")
@XmlSeeAlso({ObjectFactory.class})


public interface SampleEndpoint {

    @WebResult(name = "return", targetNamespace = "")
    @RequestWrapper(localName = "process", targetNamespace = "http://custom.binding.ns/",
className = "client.Process")
    @WebMethod
    @ResponseWrapper(localName = "processResponse", targetNamespace =
"http://custom.binding.ns/", className = "client.ProcessResponse")
    public java.lang.String process(@WebParam(name = "arg0", targetNamespace = "") String
arg0);


    @WebResult(name = "return", targetNamespace = "")
    @RequestWrapper(localName = "processCustom", targetNamespace =
"http://custom.binding.ns/", className = "client.ProcessCustom")
    @WebMethod
    @ResponseWrapper(localName = "processCustomResponse", targetNamespace =
"http://custom.binding.ns/", className = "client.ProcessCustomResponse")
    public java.lang.String processCustom(@WebParam(name = "arg0", targetNamespace = "")
String arg0);
}
```

Running the testsuite (using *mvn integration-test* command) confirms the actual messages going over the wire for the two methods are very similar: here is at first a trace of the request for the *processCustom* operation:

```
<soap:Envelope xmlns:soap="http://schemas.xmlsoap.org/soap/envelope/">
  <soap:Body>
    <ns2:process xmlns:ns2="http://custom.binding.ns/">
      <arg0>Foo-45</arg0>
    </ns2:process>
  </soap:Body>
</soap:Envelope>
```

And here is the corresponding response for the *processCustom* operation:

```
<soap:Envelope xmlns:soap="http://schemas.xmlsoap.org/soap/envelope/">
  <soap:Body>
    <ns2:processResponse xmlns:ns2="http://custom.binding.ns/">
      <return>Foo-45</return>
    </ns2:processResponse>
  </soap:Body>
</soap:Envelope>
```

Now you can compare the XML going over the wire when a custom Java model is used; At first the request:

```
<soap:Envelope xmlns:soap="http://schemas.xmlsoap.org/soap/envelope/">
  <soap:Body>
    <ns2:processCustom xmlns:ns2="http://custom.binding.ns/">
      <arg0>Bar-34</arg0>
    </ns2:processCustom>
  </soap:Body>
</soap:Envelope>
```

And here is the corresponding *processCustomResponse*:

```
<soap:Envelope xmlns:soap="http://schemas.xmlsoap.org/soap/envelope/">
  <soap:Body>
    <ns2:processCustomResponse xmlns:ns2="http://custom.binding.ns/">
```

```
        <return>Bar-34</return>
    </ns2:processCustomResponse>
  </soap:Body>
</soap:Envelope>
```

Fault handling

WSDL contracts allow defining **fault messages** to be returned to clients under specific endpoint exceptional conditions. Such fault messages are mapped to Java beans using JAXB; then the endpoint methods declare checked exceptions, which are annotated using **@javax.xml.ws.WebFault** and wrap those Java beans.

When developing a Web Service application through the **contract-first** approach, fault messages in the WSDL are automatically converted into proper Java exception classes.

The *exception-sample* project shows how to simply declare and use checked exception with a code-first approach and have them converted into proper fault messages. Unless fine-tuning of fault schema is required, the user does not need to spend time with JAXB annotations and such; he/she can simply let the tools deal with that.

As usual, the project is quickly created using the *jaxws-codefirst* Maven archetype; the included *HelloWorld* example is enriched by defining a custom **com.itbuzzpress.UnknownPersonException**:

```
package com.itbuzzpress;

public class UnknownPersonException extends Exception {
        private String name;
        private String surname;

        public UnknownPersonException() {
                super();
        }
        public UnknownPersonException(String message) {
                super(message);
        }
```

```
        public UnknownPersonException(Person person) {
                super("Unknown person '" + person.getName() + "'");
                this.name = person.getName();
                this.surname = person.getSurname();
        }
        public String getName() {
                return name;
        }
        public void setName(String name) {
                this.name = name;
        }
        public String getSurname() {
                return surname;
        }
        public void setSurname(String surname) {
                this.surname = surname;
        }
}
```

 Please note the exception class has an empty constructor and the (optional) fields have corresponding getter and setter methods.

The custom exception is declared as a checked exception in both the endpoint implementation and interface. Here is the interface class:

```
package com.itbuzzpress;

import javax.jws.WebService;

@WebService(targetNamespace = "http://hello.world.ns/")
public interface HelloWorld {
    String sayHi(String text);
    String greetings(Person person) throws UnknownPersonException;
}
```

The Web Service interface is implemented in the following *HelloWorldImpl* class, which follows here:

```
package com.itbuzzpress;

import javax.jws.WebService;
import javax.jws.soap.*;

@WebService(endpointInterface = "com.itbuzzpress.HelloWorld",
            targetNamespace = "http://hello.world.ns/",
            name = "HelloWorld",
            serviceName = "HelloWorldService",
            portName = "HelloWorldPort")
@SOAPBinding(style = Style.DOCUMENT, use = Use.LITERAL)
public class HelloWorldImpl implements HelloWorld {
    public String sayHi(String text) {
        return "Hello " + text;
    }
    public String greetings(Person person) throws UnknownPersonException {
        if (person == null) {
            throw new IllegalArgumentException("Person is null!");
        }
        if (!person.getName().equals("John") && !person.getName().equals("Alice")) {
            throw new UnknownPersonException(person);
        }
        return "Greetings " + person.getName() + " " + person.getSurname();
    }
}
```

As you can see, the *greetings(Person person)* method is throwing the checked exception when the parameter's name is not "John" or "Alice"; on the other hand, when the person parameter it's null an unchecked *IllegalArgumentException* is thrown.

The project is built and the endpoint application deployed to WildFly, through the usual *mvn wildfly:deploy* command. As part of the build, the *wsprovide* plugin generates a JAXB annotated bean for the checked exception, which is also automatically included in the deployment:

```java
package com.itbuzzpress.jaxws;
import javax.xml.bind.annotation.*;


@XmlRootElement(name = "UnknownPersonException", namespace = "http://itbuzzpress.com/")
@XmlAccessorType(XmlAccessType.FIELD)
@XmlType(name = "UnknownPersonException", namespace = "http://itbuzzpress.com/", propOrder
= {"message", "name", "surname"})
public class UnknownPersonExceptionBean {
    private java.lang.String message;
    private java.lang.String name;
    private java.lang.String surname;

    public java.lang.String getMessage() {
        return this.message;
    }
    public void setMessage(java.lang.String newMessage)  {
        this.message = newMessage;
    }
    public java.lang.String getName() {
        return this.name;
    }
    public void setName(java.lang.String newName)  {
        this.name = newName;
    }
    public java.lang.String getSurname() {
        return this.surname;
    }
    public void setSurname(java.lang.String newSurname)  {
        this.surname = newSurname;
    }
}
```

To try the sample, the *HelloWorldIntegrationTest* is modified as below, using the classes generated by **wsconsume**:

```
public class HelloWorldIntegrationTest {
    @Test
    public void testHelloWorld() throws Exception {
        HelloWorldService service = new HelloWorldService(new
URL("http://localhost:8080/exception-sample/HelloWorldService?wsdl"));
        HelloWorld port = service.getHelloWorldPort();
        Assert.assertEquals("Hello John", port.sayHi("John"));
        Person p = new Person();
        p.setName("Alice");
        p.setSurname("Li");
        Assert.assertEquals("Greetings Alice Li", port.greetings(p));
        p.setName("Mary");
        try {
            port.greetings(p);
            Assert.fail("Exception expected!");
        } catch (UnknownPersonException_Exception e) {
            Assert.assertEquals("Unknown person 'Mary'", e.getMessage());
            Assert.assertEquals("Mary", e.getFaultInfo().getName());
            Assert.assertEquals("Li", e.getFaultInfo().getSurname());
        }
        try {
            port.greetings(null);
            Assert.fail("Exception expected!");
        } catch (SOAPFaultException e) {
            Assert.assertEquals("Person is null!", e.getCause().getMessage());
        }
    }
}
```

As you can see, the *UnknownPersonException_Exception* class is intercepted in the client code; that's the exception type generated on client side by the wsdl-to-java tool; it is annotated with **@WebFault** and it wraps (as fault info) a JAXB annotated bean. Such a bean is basically the same as the one previously generated on server side and brings the information on the exception / fault to the client (in this case, the *name* and *surname*).

If a null parameter is passed to the client for the invocation, the sample server endpoint throws an unchecked exception. The JAX-WS stack converts such an exception into a generic SOAP fault, which eventually results in a *SOAPFaultException* being thrown on client side. This kind of fault is not included at all in the WSDL contract.

The test client can be run using the *mvn integration-test* command.

Finally, you can have a look at how the two exception types are mapped to SOAP messages going on the wire; the checked exception is converted into a declared **SOAP fault**:

```
<soap:Envelope xmlns:soap="http://schemas.xmlsoap.org/soap/envelope/">
  <soap:Body>
    <soap:Fault>
      <faultcode>soap:Server</faultcode>
      <faultstring>Unknown person 'Mary'</faultstring>
      <detail>
        <ns1:UnknownPersonException xmlns:ns1="http://hello.world.ns/">
          <surname xmlns:ns2="http://hello.world.ns/">Li</surname>
          <name xmlns:ns2="http://hello.world.ns/">Mary</name>
        </ns1:UnknownPersonException>
      </detail>
    </soap:Fault>
  </soap:Body>
</soap:Envelope>
```

Conversely, the unchecked exception is converted into a generic **SOAP fault**:

```
<soap:Envelope xmlns:soap="http://schemas.xmlsoap.org/soap/envelope/">
  <soap:Body>
    <soap:Fault>
      <faultcode>soap:Server</faultcode>
      <faultstring>Person is null!</faultstring>
    </soap:Fault>
  </soap:Body>
</soap:Envelope>
```

Chapter 4: WildFly JAX-WS Provider

This chapter provides information on how the JAX-WS specification is implemented in WildFly. While users can certainly rely on the vanilla server configuration, a good grasp of the various layers building up WildFly's Web Services stack allows better configuration and tuning. This chapter will cover:

- An introduction to the Web Services components of WildFly

- A brief description of the most common configuration options

- How to update the Web Services components on WildFly

- How to make direct use of some specific Web Services components (Apache CXF) and how that relates to and affects application portability.

In few words, this chapter provides a lot of advanced information on configuring both WildFly and your applications to achieve correct behavior and good performances in complex environments.

WildFly Web Services components

From a functional point of view, WildFly can be seen as a group of subsystems, exposing functionalities in multiple areas. Subsystems can be enabled or disabled depending on the configuration selected when booting the server.

The *webservices* subsystem is enabled by default in all the standalone and domain configurations included in the server. It can of course be disabled completely (by editing the relevant server configuration file) or for specific deployments only, by including a proper *jboss-deployment-structure.xml* descriptor as in the following example:

```
<jboss-deployment-structure xmlns="urn:jboss:deployment-structure:1.2">
  <deployment>
    <exclude-subsystems>
      <subsystem name="webservices" />
    </exclude-subsystems>
  </deployment>
</jboss-deployment-structure>
```

When enabled, the webservices subsystem processes any user deployment to detect and start JAX-WS endpoints.

Web Services stack libraries

Each time you deploy an application containing a Web Service endpoint, the whole Web Services stack of the server is involved; in the following sections, we will see the logical components that make up the Web Services stack which are depicted in the following snapshot:

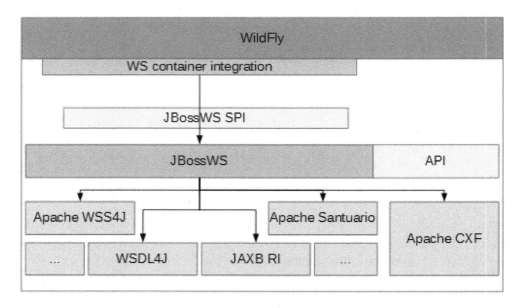

Apache CXF libraries

Apache CXF is an open source services framework. It allows building and developing services using frontend programming APIs (including JAX-WS), with services speaking a variety of protocols such as SOAP and XML/HTTP over a variety of transports such as HTTP and JMS. Apache CXF, however, is a standalone framework, which needs another component of the stack, named **JBossWS** in order to integrate with WildFly server and make it possible to use all the Web Services features included in JavaEE specifications.

JBossWS integration

JBossWS is an open source project originally started to implement JavaEE specifications for usage on JBoss AS and currently turned into an integration layer of Apache CXF into JBoss AS and WildFly. The API in the project reacts to WildFly deployments and Web Services requests by building up, configuring and running Apache CXF components. Moreover, it includes an additional user API (JBossWS API) with few annotations and interfaces providing final users with additional features beyond what's in Apache CXF. Finally, JBossWS defines **internal interfaces** (JBossWS SPI) that allow the server container to be properly decoupled from the actual Web Service libraries (namely Apache CXF) implementation details.

WildFly container integration

The WildFly container integration implements part of the JBossWS SPI to call into the core of Web Services stack when starting deployments and processing requests. Moreover, it exposes some JBossWS configuration options into the WildFly management.

Additional third-party libraries

Multiple additional third-party libraries (like Apache WSS4J, Apache Santuario, WSDL4J, JAXB RI, etc.) complete the stack, serving specific functionalities.

WildFly Modules

The group of libraries composing WildFly is organized into modules, each of them including a *module.xml* descriptor, defining a properly isolated classloader and usually including dependencies to other modules. The above-mentioned Web Service stack libraries are split into multiple modules; in particular the *org.apache.cxf.** modules contain most of the Apache CXF project archives, the *org.jboss.ws.** modules contain the JBossWS integration and the *org.jboss.as.webservices.** modules contain the WildFly container integration.

Users should not modify the *module.xml* descriptor for those modules. However, in some scenarios the user might need to declare a dependency to such modules in his deployment, to have visibility on classes from libraries that are not exposed to the final user by default. That can be achieved using a proper *jboss-deployment-structure.xml* descriptor or simply by adding a *Dependencies* entry to the deployment *MANIFEST.MF*:

```
Manifest-Version: 1.0
Dependencies: org.jboss.ws.cxf.jbossws-cxf-client services export,foo.bar
```

Below are few of the most noteworthy dependencies users might be setting:

Client side WS aggregation module

By default, the JBossWS API classes are the only part of Web Services stack that is visible to user deployment (apart from the JavaEE API, of course, which is always available, including JAX-WS). Whenever you want to use all the JBoss Web Services feature/functionalities, you can set a dependency to the convenient client module:

```
Dependencies: org.jboss.ws.cxf.jbossws-cxf-client services
```

Please note the *services* option above: that's strictly required in order to get proper JBossWS version of classes that are retrieved using the Java Service API.

Apache CXF API

In order to use the Apache CXF specific API, the following dependency is to be set:

```
Dependencies: org.apache.cxf
```

Configuring the Web Services subsystem

The webservices subsystem offers some configuration options mainly in two areas:

- The published endpoint address rewrite
- The predefined client endpoint configurations.

The sections below describe them and explain how to configure the subsystem according to your needs. The webservices subsystem can be modified and managed just like the other WildFly subsystems, that is, by manually editing the *standalone.xml* or *domain.xml* files, using the command line interface or using the web console.

Address rewrite

Each time an endpoint is deployed, the webservices subsystem processes its WSDL contract, if provided, or generates one from scratch for it, if not provided. The WSDL contains a *{http://schemas.xmlsoap.org/wsdl/soap/}address* (*soap:address*) element for each endpoint. That element has a *location* attribute, which informs the container where to send SOAP messages to for invoking the endpoint:

```
<soap:address location="https://exampleserver.com/services/ExampleService" />
```

Due to the relevance of that piece of the contract, JBossWS has a mechanism for rewriting such element according to configuration options in the webservices subsystem.

```
<subsystem xmlns="urn:jboss:domain:webservices:1.2"
xmlns:javaee="http://java.sun.com/xml/ns/javaee"
    xmlns:jaxwsconfig="urn:jboss:jbossws-jaxws-config:4.0">
    <wsdl-host>localhost</wsdl-host>
    <modify-wsdl-address>true</modify-wsdl-address>
    <wsdl-port>8080</wsdl-port>
    <wsdl-secure-port>8443</wsdl-secure-port>
</subsystem>
```

With a configuration as this, the **soap:address** mentioned above would result in the following one in the published contract:

```
<soap:address location="https://localhost:8443/services/ExampleService" />
```

Let's see more in details what each element of the configuration actually controls.

modify-wsdl-address

The *modify-wsdl-address* element is used to enable and disable the address rewrite functionality. The address rewrite mechanism is triggered automatically regardless of the *modify-wsdl-address* value when the soap:address element in the provided WSDL has an invalid URL specified in the *location* attribute. The stack will simply set the address of the actually published endpoint.

Otherwise, a *true* value for *modify-wsdl-address* will make JBossWS rewrite the *soap:address location* attribute value by replacing the host and port of the specified URL address with the values from the *wsdl-host*, *wsdl-port* (or *wsdl-secure-port* for *https* protocol) configuration elements.

wsdl-host

The *wsdl-host* element defines the hostname or IP address to be used for rewriting the *soap:address location* attributes. If *modify-wsdl-address* is set *true* and the *wsdl-host* element is not defined or set to *jbossws.undefined.host*, WildFly will rewrite the location address using the requester host from the WSDL retrieval call. This is useful in some scenarios when the WildFly server is running behind a load-balancer or other type of server exposing WildFly on different (public) IP addresses.

wsdl-port

The *wsdl-port* element is used to define explicitly a port number that will be used for rewriting *soap:address location* attributes of endpoints exposed over *http* protocol.

wsdl-secure-port

The *wsdl-secure-port* element is used to explicitly define a port number that will be used for rewriting *soap:address location* attributes of endpoints exposed over *https* protocol.

Predefined client and endpoint configurations

JBossWS enables extra setup configuration data to be predefined and associated with endpoints and clients. Each configuration can include JAX-WS handlers and key/value properties declarations to control JBossWS and Apache CXF internals. Configurations can be defined in the webservices subsystem and in a deployment descriptor file within the application.

Predefined configuration contents

Each endpoint configuration may be associated with zero or more *PRE* and *POST* handler chains. Each handler chain may include JAX-WS handlers, which can be executed according to the following rules:

- For **outbound messages,** the *PRE* handler chains are executed *before* any handler attached to the endpoint (for example by means of a *@HandlerChain* annotation) whilst *POST* handler chains are triggered *after* endpoint handlers have executed.

- For **inbound messages**, the opposite applies: the *POST* handler chains are executed before any handler that is attached to the endpoint using the standard means, while the *PRE* handler chains are executed afterwards.

The same handler chain execution ordering applies to client configurations.

Besides handlers, a predefined configuration can also include multiple key/value properties for controlling JBossWS and Apache CXF internals.

Assigning configurations to endpoints

The annotation *org.jboss.ws.api.annotation.EndpointConfig* can be used to specify that a JAX-WS endpoint is to be assigned a given configuration. When assigning a configuration that is defined in the webservices subsystem, the configuration name is the only required piece of information. On the opposite, when assigning a configuration that is defined in the application, the relative path to the deployment descriptor and the configuration name must be specified, as in the following code:

```
@EndpointConfig(configFile = "WEB-INF/my-endpoint-config.xml", configName = "Custom
Endpoint")
public class MyServiceImpl implements MyService {
    public String helloworld() {
        return "Hello World!";
    }
}
```

Below is an example of the referenced configuration file, which must be located in **WEB-INF** or **META-INF** folder of the deployment depending on it being a war or jar archive. The XML schema for the descriptor can be found online at http://anonsvn.jboss.org/repos/jbossws/spi/tags/jbossws-spi-2.1.0.Final/src/main/resources/schema/jbossws-jaxws-config_4_0.xsd :

```
<jaxws-config xmlns="urn:jboss:jbossws-jaxws-config:4.0"
xmlns:xsi="http://www.w3.org/2001/XMLSchema-instance"
xmlns:javaee="http://java.sun.com/xml/ns/javaee"
                xsi:schemaLocation="urn:jboss:jbossws-jaxws-config:4.0 jaxws-config_2_0.xsd">
    <endpoint-config>
        <config-name>Custom Server Config</config-name>
        <post-handler-chains>
            <javaee:handler-chain>
                <javaee:handler>
                    <javaee:handler-name>CustomHandler1</javaee:handler-name>
                    <javaee:handler-class>com.itbuzzpress.foo.CustomHandler</javaee:handler-
class>
                </javaee:handler>
            </javaee:handler-chain>
        </post-handler-chains>
        <pre-handler-chains>
            <javaee:handler-chain>
                <javaee:handler>
                    <javaee:handler-name>CustomHandler2</javaee:handler-name>
                    <javaee:handler-
class>com.itbuzzpress.foo.AnotherCustomHandler</javaee:handler-class>
```

```
        </javaee:handler>
      </javaee:handler-chain>
    </pre-handler-chains>
    <property>
        <property-name>schema-validation-enabled</property-name>
        <property-value>true</property-value>
    </property>
  </endpoint-config>
</jaxws-config>
```

Assigning configurations to clients

JAX-WS clients can be assigned JBossWS configurations programmatically using *org.jboss.ws.api.configuration.ClientConfigFeature*, an extension to the JAX-WS *javax.xml.ws.WebServiceFeature*.

```
import org.jboss.ws.api.configuration.ClientConfigFeature;


Service service = Service.create(wsdlURL, serviceName);
Endpoint port = service.getPort(Endpoint.class, new ClientConfigFeature("META-INF/jaxws-client-config.xml", "Custom Client Config"));
port.echo("Kermit");
//... or ....
port = service.getPort(Endpoint.class, new ClientConfigFeature("META-INF/jaxws-client-config.xml", "Custom Client Config"), true); //setup properties too from the configuration
port.echo("Kermit");
//... or ...
port = service.getPort(Endpoint.class, new ClientConfigFeature(null, testConfigName));
//reads from current container configurations if available
port.echo("Kermit");
```

JBossWS parses the specified configuration file. The configuration file must be found as a resource by the classloader of the current thread; the link to the XML schema is the same mentioned above for the endpoint configurations.

Defining configurations in the webservices subsystem

Now that the concept of client and endpoint configurations has been introduced, let's see how to add predefined container level configurations (available to all deployed applications) by modifying the WildFly webservices subsystem.

The schema (https://github.com/wildfly/wildfly/blob/8.0.0.Final/build/src/main/resources/docs/schema/jboss-as-webservices_1_2.xsd) for the **webservices** subsystem allows using the same **endpoint-config** and **client-config** elements that are used in external files included in the deployments:

```
<subsystem xmlns="urn:jboss:domain:webservices:1.2">
  <endpoint-config name="Standard-Endpoint-Config"/>
  <endpoint-config name="Recording-Endpoint-Config">
    <pre-handler-chain name="recording-handlers" protocol-bindings="##SOAP11_HTTP
##SOAP11_HTTP_MTOM ##SOAP12_HTTP ##SOAP12_HTTP_MTOM">
      <handler name="RecordingHandler"
class="org.jboss.ws.common.invocation.RecordingServerHandler"/>
    </pre-handler-chain>
  </endpoint-config>
  <client-config name="Standard-Client-Config"/>
</subsystem>
```

The predefined configurations concept allows transparently adding a handler to any client or endpoint. In order to be able to successfully load the handler class, the deployment, which uses the predefined configuration, needs to have visibility over the module containing the handler class. Therefore, proper JBoss Module dependencies might have to be specified (in the MANIFEST.MF of the deployment, for example). The handler classes from the JBossWS components are automatically resolved.

Standard configurations

In the above excerpt of the webservices subsystem, you can see two special configurations: *Standard-Client-Config* and *Standard-Endpoint-Config*. Those are the predefined client and endpoint configurations which are assigned when you didn't set any configuration for them. This gives administrators a chance to tune default handler chains for any client and endpoints.

Web Services deployment descriptors

It has been previously demonstrated that it is possible to deploy JAX-WS endpoints on WildFly without any mandatory deployment descriptor. However, JBossWS (and hence WildFly) supports few optional descriptors to control and customize deployments processing.

web.xml

A common *web.xml* descriptor can be used within WEB-INF folder of a *war* deployment to configure the *url-pattern* for the addresses of JAX-WS POJO endpoints included in the archive. Here is an example of the expected content of *web.xml*:

```
<web-app xmlns:xsi="http://www.w3.org/2001/XMLSchema-instance"
xmlns="http://xmlns.jcp.org/xml/ns/javaee"
xsi:schemaLocation="http://xmlns.jcp.org/xml/ns/javaee
http://xmlns.jcp.org/xml/ns/javaee/web-app_3_1.xsd" id="WebApp_ID" version="3.1">

  <servlet>

    <servlet-name>TestService</servlet-name>

    <servlet-class>com.itbuzzpress.foo.MyEndpoint</servlet-class>

  </servlet>
  <servlet-mapping>

    <servlet-name>TestService</servlet-name>

    <url-pattern>/*</url-pattern>

  </servlet-mapping>
</web-app>
```

com.itbuzzpress.foo.MyEndpoint is the full qualified name of the endpoint class annotated with *@WebService* / *@WebServiceProvider*. A *servlet - servlet-mapping* couple of tags needs to be provided for each endpoint in the deployment.

 Technically speaking the class annotated with *@WebService* / *@WebServiceProvider* is not a Servlet class, and is not to be annotated with *@WebServlet* either. The WildFly integration will be processing the above *web.xml* descriptor at deploy time and will rewrite it properly in memory for the undertow subsystem, having detected the specified endpoint class.

jboss-webservices.xml

For those willing to configure a given Web Services endpoint deployment without adding a compile time dependency to WildFly (or Apache CXF) specific classes, the *jboss-webservices.xml* descriptor can be also used. It needs to be placed either in *WEB-INF* or *META-INF* folder of the deployment (depending on it being a *war* or *jar* archive) and is structured as follows:

```
<webservices xmlns="http://www.jboss.com/xml/ns/javaee" version="1.2">
  <context-root/>?
  <config-name/>?
  <config-file/>?
  <property>*
    <name/>
    <value/>
  </property>
  <port-component>*
    <ejb-name/>
    <port-component-name/>
    <port-component-uri/>?
    <auth-method/>?
    <transport-guarantee/>?
    <secure-wsdl-access/>?
  </port-component>
</webservices>
```

Let's see in detail each element that makeup the **jboss-webservices.xml** descriptor:

context-root element

The *context-root* element can be used to customize the context root of the web application that is being deployed.

```
<webservices>
  <context-root>my-context-root</context-root>
</webservices>
```

config-name and config-file elements

The *config-name* and *config-file* elements can be used to associate any endpoint provided in the deployment with a given endpoint configuration. Endpoint configurations are specified either in a referenced config file or in the webservices subsystem section of the WildFly management model. The example below is from a *jar* archive containing EJB3 endpoint(s); the *custom.xml* config file is referenced and will have to be included in *META-INF* folder of the deployment archive.

```
<webservices>
  <config-name>My Custom Endpoint</config-name>
  <config-file>META-INF/custom.xml</config-file>
</webservices>
```

property element

The property elements can be used to setup context property to configure the WS stack behavior.

```
<property>
  <name>prop.name</name>
  <value>prop.value</value>
</property>
```

Among the supported properties, there are some JBossWS defined ones that control Apache CXF integration without requiring Apache CXF API direct usage in the deployment. Check the <u>wiki</u> for additional information about it.

port-component element

The *port-component* element can be used to customize the endpoint address for EJB3 endpoints or to configure security related properties.

```
<webservices>
  <port-component>
    <ejb-name>TestService</ejb-name>
    <port-component-name>TestServicePort</port-component-name>
    <port-component-uri>/*</port-component-uri>
    <auth-method>BASIC</auth-method>
    <transport-guarantee>NONE</transport-guarantee>
    <secure-wsdl-access>true</secure-wsdl-access>
  </port-component>
</webservices>
```

Example usage

As an example of *jboss-webservices.xml* usage, we'll be controlling the way Apache CXF deals with **WS-Policy** alternatives for incoming messages.

 A **WS-Policy** represents a set of specifications that describe the capabilities and constraints of the security policies on intermediaries and endpoints. It also deals with how to associate policies with services and endpoints.

Have a look at the following WS-Policy example, featuring a policy having two alternatives:

```
<wsp:Policy>
  <wsp:ExactlyOne>
    <wsp:Policy>
      <wswa:UsingAddressing xmlns:wswa="http://www.w3.org/2006/05/addressing/wsdl"/>
    </wsp:Policy>
    <wsp:Policy>
      <wswa:UsingAddressing xmlns:wswa="http://www.w3.org/2006/05/addressing/wsdl"/>
      <wsrmp:RMAssertion xmlns:wsrmp="http://schemas.xmlsoap.org/ws/2005/02/rm/policy"/>
    </wsp:Policy>
  </wsp:ExactlyOne>
</wsp:Policy>
```

When the Apache CXF policy engine processes incoming messages on the server side, it needs a strategy to select a policy alternative if multiple ones are valid for the received message. In the example above, a message using both WS-Addressing and WS-ReliableMessaging would actually match both policy alternative requirements.

The selection task is performed by a CXF component named *AlternativeSelector*. The JBossWS integration defaults to *org.apache.cxf.ws.policy.selector.MaximalAlternativeSelector* implementation, which chooses the alternative with most assertions (in the example, that's the second alternative, of course, as it has two assertions, while the first just has one).

For complex policies, the default behavior might not always be the proper solution, so users might want a different strategy to be applied for a given deployment. That is achieved by including a *jboss-webservices.xml* descriptor as follows in the deployment:

```
<webservices
  xmlns="http://www.jboss.com/xml/ns/javaee"
  xmlns:xsi="http://www.w3.org/2001/XMLSchema-instance"
  version="1.2"
  xsi:schemaLocation="http://www.jboss.com/xml/ns/javaee">
  <property>
    <name>cxf.policy.alternativeSelector</name>
    <value>org.apache.cxf.ws.policy.selector.MinimalAlternativeSelector</value>
  </property>
</webservices>
```

Modifying the Web Services stack

Under some circumstances, you might want to modify the Web Services stack, the most common reason being the need for a newer version of a library.

Upgrading the JBossWS stack

Generally speaking, replacing a library included in one of the application server modules brings some risks and is hence discouraged. When it comes to the Web Services stack, though, the WildFly developers can leverage the community releases of the JBossWS project.

After having downloaded and decompressed the JBossWS binary distribution archive from the http://www.jboss.org/jbossws website, you have to copy the *ant.properties.example* file into *ant.properties* and edit it providing the actual location of your WildFly instance:

```
wildfly800.home=/dati/wildfly-8.0.0.Final
jbossws.integration.target=wildfly800
```

Then the installation is triggered by the following Ant command:

```
ant deploy-wildfly800
```

This assumes you're installing JBossWS on top of WildFly 8.0.0.Final. Please note each JBossWS version has a set of supported target containers; the website clearly tells which they are.

At the end of the Ant script processing, the target WildFly instance is upgraded; all the libraries included in the JBossWS binary distribution are copied to the proper locations within the application server directory, the old versions removed and the module descriptors are updated.

 The advantage of relying on the JBossWS binary distribution install is that the included libraries have been tested and verified all together before the release, in order to avoid regressions and cut down the upgrade risks.

Installing Spring on WildFly

Installing Spring libraries is not mandatory to get working with Web Services on WildFly as the Web Services stack does not depend on the **Spring framework** (despite internally relying on the Apache CXF engine). In some cases, however, the user might still want to use Spring-based descriptors for declaring endpoints and hence need Spring to be available.

For the Web Services stack to have correct visibility over Spring classes, the Spring libraries need to be properly installed in a specific WildFly module, the *org.springframework.spring* module, which many Web Services stack modules on the server already have optional dependencies to.

Installing Spring libraries in that module is basically a matter of copying the Spring jars in the correct path (*JBOSS_HOME/modules/org/springframework/spring/main*) which needs to be at first created, and adding its *module.xml* descriptor.

Below is an example of the Spring *module.xml*, containing the name of jars referenced in the *resource-root* paths, which must match the actual name of the jars in the module:

```
<module xmlns="urn:jboss:module:1.1" name="org.springframework.spring">
    <resources>
        <resource-root path="spring-core.jar"/>
        <resource-root path="spring-beans.jar"/>
        <resource-root path="spring-jms.jar"/>
        <resource-root path="spring-context.jar"/>
        <resource-root path="spring-asm.jar"/>
        <resource-root path="spring-expression.jar"/>
        <resource-root path="spring-tx.jar"/>
        <resource-root path="spring-aop.jar"/>
```

```
    </resources>
    <dependencies>
        <module name="javax.api" />
        <module name="javax.jms.api" />
        <module name="javax.annotation.api" />
        <module name="org.apache.commons.logging" />
        <module name="org.jboss.vfs" />
    </dependencies>
</module>
```

An alternative to manually creating the *org.springframework.spring* module is to rely on the JBossWS binary distribution install script. That is particularly convenient if the WS stack already needs to be upgraded for different reasons. When invoking the Ant script, after having provided a proper *ant.properties* file as explained in the previous section of this chapter, the *-Dspring=true* option can be used to have the *org.springframework.spring* created on the application server:

```
ant -Dspring=true deploy-wildfly800
```

WildFly and Apache CXF

JAX-WS features have been introduced in the previous chapters and it has been shown how to build applications making use of them on the WildFly application server. It has also been explained that the Web Services stack providing those JAX-WS functionalities in WildFly is internally based on the **Apache CXF libraries**, which are connected to the various WildFly components through the JBossWS integration.

To summarize, the JBossWS integration layer is mainly meant for:

- Allowing using standard webservices APIs (including JAX-WS) on WildFly; this is performed internally leveraging Apache CXF without requiring the user to deal with or directly rely on it;

- Allowing using Apache CXF advanced features (including WS-*) on top of WildFly without requiring the user to deal with / setup / care about the required integration steps for running in such a container.

Building WS applications: the JBoss way

The Apache CXF client and endpoint configuration is deeply based on Spring and relies on a configuration file named *cxf.xml*; this file may contain any basic Bean plus specific WS client and endpoint Beans which CXF has custom parsers for. For the sake of understanding, below is an example of such a *cxf.xml*:

```xml
<beans xmlns='http://www.springframework.org/schema/beans'
       xmlns:xsi='http://www.w3.org/2001/XMLSchema-instance'
       xmlns:beans='http://www.springframework.org/schema/beans'
       xmlns:jaxws='http://cxf.apache.org/jaxws'
       xmlns:cxf='http://cxf.apache.org/core'
       xsi:schemaLocation='http://www.springframework.org/schema/beans
               http://www.springframework.org/schema/beans/spring-beans.xsd
               http://cxf.apache.org/jaxws
               http://cxf.apache.org/schemas/jaxws.xsd
               http://cxf.apache.org/core
               http://cxf.apache.org/schemas/core.xsd'>
  <jaxws:endpoint id="helloWorldServiceEndpoint"
                  address="http://localhost:8080/foo/helloworld"
                  implementor="#helloWorldServiceBean">
  </jaxws:endpoint>
  <bean id="testBean" class="foo.TestBean" />
  <bean id="helloWorldServiceBean" class="foo.HelloWorldService">
    <constructor-arg ref="testBean" />
  </bean>
</beans>
```

Apache CXF can be used to deploy Web Service endpoints on any Servlet container by including its libraries in the deployment; in such a scenario, Spring basically serves as a convenient configuration option, given direct Apache CXF API usage won't be very handy. Similar reasoning applies on client side, where a Spring based descriptor offers a shortcut for setting up Apache CXF internals.

This said, nowadays almost any Apache CXF functionality can be configured and used through direct API usage, without Spring.

Hence, when building an application meant to run on WildFly, the user should not provide Spring *cxf.xml* descriptors based on the assumption that those descriptors will be automatically processed during deployment. WildFly internally relies on some of the Apache CXF libraries, but it does not expose Apache CXF configuration approach (based on Spring) by default. There are multiple reasons for such a choice, basically related to the need for offering a full JavaEE container implementation, which is different from the Apache CXF project goals.

Portable applications

Actually, WildFly is much more than a Servlet container; it actually provides users with a fully compliant target platform for Java EE applications.

Generally speaking, users are encouraged to write portable applications; when it comes to Web Services, that means relying only on JAX-WS specification whenever possible. That is what has been explained and covered with examples in the previous chapters of this book. Writing JAX-WS standard applications ensures easy migrations to and from compliant platforms. The container, here WildFly, takes care of serving JAX-WS features with its own implementation; that means the user does not need to embed any Apache CXF or any ws-related dependency library in its JAX-WS standard deployments.

WS-* enabled applications

The JAX-WS specification (as well as any other specification that is part of JavaEE) does not cover **WS-* usage** (WS-Security, WS-Addressing, WS-ReliableMessaging, etc).

 The WS-Specifications build a compound architecture to form an environment for complex Web Service applications.

In short, that means there's no standard API for setting up those WS additional technologies. However, at the WSDL contract level, those can all be configured in a standard way using WS-Policy assertions.

To favor portability, the WildFly preferred solution for developing WS-* enabled applications is hence to use the **contract-first** (top-down) approach and start with WSDL documents properly describing the services additional requirements through WS-Security, WS-ReliableMessaging, etc. policy assertions.

Apache CXF has a WS-Policy engine whose configuration can be completely driven by WS-Policy assertions. The information that is not conveyed by the contract can be provided through context properties. The JBossWS integration exposes WS-* functionalities on WildFly by relying on the WS-Policy engine of Apache CXF and requiring users to only specify the few context properties that are needed; in most of the cases, there's no actual need for making direct usage of Apache CXF internal API or Spring descriptors.

Direct Apache CXF API usage

Whenever users can't really meet their application requirements with JAX-WS plus WS-Policy, it is of course still possible to rely on direct Apache CXF API usage (given that's included in the AS), at the price of losing the Java EE portability of the application. That could be the case of a user needing specific Apache CXF functionalities, or having to consume WS-* enabled endpoints which are advertised through legacy WSDL contracts without WS-Policy assertions.

To make use of Apache CXF API, a module dependency to *org.apache.cxf module* (and possibly to *org.apache.cxf.impl* module) is required for the user deployment. See the previous sections for details on how to declare that.

 A dependency to *org.apache.cxf* module is also required when Apache CXF annotations (like @InInterceptor, @Gzip, ...) are used on endpoints and handlers classes. Without that, the annotations are simply ignored by WildFly.

JBossWS API and deployment descriptors usage

As previously mentioned, the JBossWS API adds few additional features and configuration options on top of what comes with plain Apache CXF.

 The JBossWS API is automatically available to WildFly deployments and no module dependency needs to be explicitly specified for it.

The most relevant classes in JBossWS API are used for setting default configurations on endpoints (*org.jboss.ws.api.annotation.EndpointConfig* annotation) and on clients (*org.jboss.ws.api.configuration.ClientConfigFeature* class). As mentioned above, those configurations can include context properties specification, which is used for example for WS-* setup, in conjunction with WS-Policy assertions in the WSDL contract.

Similarly, context properties can be specified in the *jboss-webservices.xml* deployment descriptor.

Apache CXF Spring descriptors usage

In some cases, users might still want to consume Spring *cxf.xml* descriptors.

On client side, in order to do that, the Spring libraries need to be available in the current thread classloader. For JAX-WS clients running in-container on WildFly, a dependency to the previously mentioned *org.springframework.spring* module is a valid solution for adding Spring to the classloader. When Spring is available, the creation of Apache CXF Bus instances will load *cxf.xml* descriptor resources that can be found using the current thread classloader.

On server side, when the *org.springframework.spring* module is properly configured, JBossWS processes a custom descriptor, which can be added to the Web Services deployments. The convention for such a descriptor is the following:

- The descriptor file name must be *jbossws-cxf.xml*

- This descriptor is located in **WEB-INF** directory for POJO deployments

- This descriptor is located in **META-INF** for EJB3 deployments

The *jbossws-cxf.xml* is parsed similarly to a common *cxf.xml* in order for building up an Apache CXF Bus instance for the WS deployment; the endpoint beans included in the deployment are to be specified using the *<jaxws:endpoint>* tag the same they would be specified in a *cxf.xml* descriptor.

Here is an example of *jbossws-cxf.xml*, which contains an endpoint definition:

```xml
<beans
 xmlns="http://www.springframework.org/schema/beans"
 xmlns:xsi="http://www.w3.org/2001/XMLSchema-instance"
 xmlns:beans="http://www.springframework.org/schema/beans"
 xmlns:jaxws="http://cxf.apache.org/jaxws"
 xsi:schemaLocation="http://www.springframework.org/schema/beans
 http://www.springframework.org/schema/beans/spring-beans.xsd
 http://cxf.apache.org/jaxws
 http://cxf.apache.org/schemas/jaxws.xsd">
  <jaxws:endpoint id="SampleWS" address="http://localhost:8080/SampleWS"
   implementor="com.sample.SampleWS">
```

```
<jaxws:invoker>
  <bean class="org.jboss.wsf.stack.cxf.JBossWSInvoker"/>
</jaxws:invoker>
</jaxws:endpoint>
</beans>
```

Once loaded the *jbossws-cxf.xml*, the WildFly HTTP engine will be serving the endpoints.

Apache CXF Bus usage

Most of the Apache CXF features are configured using the *org.apache.cxf.Bus* class. While the Apache CXF documentation covers any detail on Bus, it is also extremely important to be aware of the implications of using Bus instances on WildFly.

Apache CXF uses static members in the *org.apache.cxf.BusFactory* class to keep references to:

- A global default Bus instance
- A thread default Bus for each thread (using a Thread to Bus map).

As previously explained, the Apache CXF libraries are contained in a given module of WildFly, defining the classloader for all classes from those libraries. Therefore, whenever relying on the *org.apache.cxf* module dependency, there's a unique **global default Bus reference** and unique map with references to a Bus instance for each thread.

The result of putting the Apache CXF Bus architecture on top of the WildFly EE container classloading mechanism is that:

- Setting and using the global default Bus instance is always to be avoided;
- Whenever a Bus instance is created using the Apache CXF API, that should eventually be destroyed or at least removed from the thread association, as threads are kept in pools and reused in-container.

Bus selection strategies for JAX-WS clients

Apache CXF Bus instances are also created internally by the JBossWS integration any time a JAX-WS client stub is needed; the client is registered within the Bus and the Bus affects the client behavior (e.g. through the configured CXF interceptors).

For the same reasons mentioned above, the way a Bus is internally selected for serving a given JAX-WS client is very important, especially for in-container clients. The following sections show the available strategies for picking up or creating a Bus which can be used by WildFly developers.

Thread bus strategy

Each time the JAX-WS API is used to create a Bus, the JBossWS integration will automatically make sure a Bus is currently associated to the current thread in the BusFactory. If that does not happen, a new Bus is created and linked to the current thread (to prevent the user from relying on the default Bus). The Apache CXF engine will then create the client using the current thread Bus. This is the default strategy; it lets users automatically reuse a previously created Bus instance and allows using customized Bus that can possibly be created and associated to the thread before building up a JAX-WS client.

The drawback of the strategy is that the tight coupling between the Bus instance and the thread which needs to be eventually cleaned up (when not needed anymore). Therefore, when relying on this strategy, the safest approach to be sure of cleaning up the link is to surround the JAX-WS client with a try/finally block as below:

```
try {
  Service service = Service.create(wsdlURL, serviceQName);  MyEndpoint port =
service.getPort(MyEndpoint.class);
  //...
} finally {
  BusFactory.setThreadDefaultBus(null);
  bus.shutdown(true);
}
```

New Bus strategy

Another strategy is to let the JBossWS integration create a new Bus each time a JAX-WS client is built. The main benefit of this approach is that a brand new Bus won't rely on any formerly cached information (e.g. cached WSDL / schemas) which might have changed after the previous client creation. The main drawback is, of course, worse performance as the Bus creation takes time.

- If there's a Bus already associated to the current thread before the JAX-WS client creation, that is automatically restored when returning control to the user; in other words, the newly created

102

Bus will be used only for the created JAX-WS client but won't stay associated to the current thread at the end of the process.

- Similarly, if the thread was not associated to any Bus before the client creation, no Bus will be associated to the thread at the end of the client creation.

Thread Context Classloader Bus strategy

The last strategy is to have the Bus created for serving the client to be associated to the **Current Thread Context Classloader (TCCL)**. That means the same Bus instance is *shared* by JAX-WS clients running when the same TCCL is set. This is particularly interesting as each web application deployment usually has its own context classloader, so this strategy allows keeping the number of created Bus instances bound to the applications number in the WildFly container.

- If there's a Bus already associated to the current thread before the JAX-WS client creation, that is automatically restored when returning control to the user. In other words, the Bus corresponding to the current thread context classloader will be used only for the newly created JAX-WS client but won't stay associated to the current thread at the end of the process.

- If the thread was not associated to any Bus before the client creation, a new Bus will be created (and later user for any other client built with this strategy and the same TCCL in place); however, no Bus will be associated to the thread at the end of the client creation.

Strategy configuration

Users can request a given Bus selection strategy to be used for the client being built by specifying one of the following JBossWS features (which extend *javax.xml.ws.WebServiceFeature*) contained in the following table:

Feature	Strategy
org.jboss.wsf.stack.cxf.client.UseThreadBusFeature	Thread bus (THREAD_BUS)
org.jboss.wsf.stack.cxf.client.UseNewBusFeature	New bus (NEW_BUS)
org.jboss.wsf.stack.cxf.client.UseTCCLBusFeature	Thread context classloader bus (TCCL_BUS)

The feature is specified as follows:

```
Service service = Service.create(wsdlURL, serviceQName, new UseThreadBusFeature());
```

If no feature is explicitly specified, the system default strategy is used, which can be modified through the *org.jboss.ws.cxf.jaxws-client.bus.strategy* system property when starting the JVM. The valid values for the property are THREAD_BUS, NEW_BUS and TCCL_BUS. The default is THREAD_BUS.

Chapter 5: Web Services Security

This chapter will introduce to the most common concerns about Web Services security. After an initial overview of the key security concepts, some common scenarios will be described through source code examples and directions on configuring the WildFly container properly.

The most relevant topics that will be covered are:

- Transport level security

- Authentication and authorization

- WS-Security and WS-Security Policy

Key security concepts

In the information technology field, security is a huge topic; thus covering all its aspects is a hard task. Speaking of Web Services, though, few security key concepts can be relied upon to describe common needs and solutions for satisfying them.

Security principles

We could say that Web Services security is ensured when the following principles are taken into account:

Authenticity

When two parties are involved in a Web Services communication, it is important to validate that both are who they claim to be. If that is not possible, the exchanged data can't always be assumed to be genuine.

Integrity

Once each party knows who he/she is communicating with, data integrity has to be ensured; in other words, the two parties need to be sure data is not altered by a third party in the middle of the communication.

Confidentiality

In some scenarios, such as when dealing with very sensible information, integrity is not enough and the sending and receiving parties also require that no other party can actually read (eavesdrop) the communication.

Non-repudiation

Finally, in some circumstances, the receiving party might need to be sure the sending party can't deny having sent a message that's been received.

Access control

The above-mentioned principles are usually coupled with some forms of access control, when messages reach the target endpoints. That is required to protect information restricting it to people who are actually authorized to access it. The process is usually composed of three steps:

Identification

The sending party needs to tell the receiving party who he/she is; that means providing some identity claim in the message, for instance a username.

Authentication

The receiving party has to verify the identity claim; the simplest way is possibly requiring the sending party to provide also a password the receiver can check.

Authorization

Finally, after the sending party has been successfully identified and authenticated, the receiver needs to check if the sender is actually authorized to access the data he's asking for in the message. Various mechanism and policies exist here; the use of security roles assigned to user profiles is one of the simplest scenarios.

Web Services access control on WildFly

As formerly explained, Web Service endpoints on WildFly are built on top of POJO or EJB3 components, which already have a built-in security mechanism based on the concept of Security Domains. Therefore, we will learn now which are the steps required for controlling access within a Security Domain.

Specifying a security domain

The first step for allowing user authentication for a given endpoint, is to associate it to an existing security domain (or define a new security domain from scratch).

Security domains are part of the WildFly *security* subsystem in the management model; within the *standalone.xml* descriptor you'd see something like this:

```xml
<subsystem xmlns="urn:jboss:domain:security:1.2">
  <security-domains>
    <security-domain name="other" cache-type="default">
      <authentication>
        <login-module code="Remoting" flag="optional">
          <module-option name="password-stacking" value="useFirstPass"/>
        </login-module>
        <login-module code="RealmDirect" flag="required">
          <module-option name="password-stacking" value="useFirstPass"/>
        </login-module>
      </authentication>
    </security-domain>
    . . . .
    <security-domain name="TestWS">
      <authentication>
        <login-module code="UsersRoles" flag="required">
          <module-option name="usersProperties" value="/foo/bar/testws-users.properties"/>
          <module-option name="unauthenticatedIdentity" value="anonymous"/>
          <module-option name="rolesProperties" value="/foo/bar/testws-roles.properties"/>
        </login-module>
      </authentication>
    </security-domain>
  </security-domains>
</subsystem>
```

The *TestWS* security-domain is there explicitly for this example and, as usual, can be added either manually editing the descriptor or using the Command Line Interface or through the web Admin console. The security-domain relies on a *UserRoles* login module, which basically performs authentication and authorization using username/password and roles. Two configuration files, mapping usernames to their corresponding passwords and roles are referenced:

testws-users.properties

```
# A sample users.properties file for use with the UsersRoles Login Module
kermit=thefrog
```

testws-roles.properties

```
# A sample roles.properties file for use with the UsersRoles Login Module
kermit=friend,foo
```

Basically, the test domain includes a user identity whose username is "kermit", whose password is "thefrog" and which has "friend" and "foo" roles.

Once the security-domain is defined, endpoints can reference it; that is achieved differently, depending on the Web Services endpoint type. EJB3 endpoints rely on the ***@org.jboss.ejb3.annotation.SecurityDomain*** annotation.

```
import javax.ejb.Stateless;
import javax.jws.WebService;
import org.jboss.ejb3.annotation.SecurityDomain;

@Stateless
@WebService (
    name = "SecureEndpoint",
    serviceName = "SecureEndpointService",
    targetNamespace = "http://org.test.ws/securityDomain"
)
@SecurityDomain("TestWS")
public class SecureEndpointImpl
{
...
}
```

POJO endpoints, instead, require that you specify the security domain in the JBoss/WildFly deployment descriptor, named *jboss-web.xml* descriptor, which is to be included in the WEB-INF directory of the deployment archive:

```
<jboss-web>
  <security-domain>TestWS</security-domain>
</jboss-web>
```

Restricting endpoint access

After having associated the endpoint with a given security domain, role requirements can be established for performing authorization. This is achieved the same way you'd do for plain EJB3 and Web applications, that is by either relying on *@RolesAllowed*, *@PermitAll*, *@DenyAll*, etc. annotations or on proper *security-constraint / security-role* blocks in the *web.xml* descriptor.

Here is for example, the EJB3 endpoint decorated with security annotations:

```
import javax.annotation.security.*;
import javax.ejb.Stateless;
import javax.jws.*;
import org.jboss.ejb3.annotation.SecurityDomain;

@Stateless
@WebService ( name = "SecureEndpoint", serviceName = "SecureEndpointService",
              targetNamespace = "http://org.jboss.ws/securityDomain"
)
@DeclareRoles({"friend", "royal"})
@SecurityDomain("TestWS")

public class SecureEndpointImpl {
    @PermitAll
    @WebMethod
    public String echoForAll(String input) {  ...   }

    @RolesAllowed("friend")
    @WebMethod
```

```
   public String echo(String input) {  ...  }

   @RolesAllowed("royal")
   @WebMethod
   public String restrictedEcho(String input) {   ...    }
}
```

The combination of *@DeclareRoles*, *@RolesAllowed* and *@PermitAll* annotations basically tells the container that two roles exists for this endpoint ("friend" and "royal"); users belonging to "friend" role can call into the *echoForAll* and *echo* methods, while users belonging to "royal" role can invoke the *echoForAll* and *restrictedEcho* methods.

A POJO endpoint would have a *web.xml* including something as follows instead:

```
<security-constraint>
  <web-resource-collection>
    <web-resource-name>All resources</web-resource-name>
    <url-pattern>/*</url-pattern>
  </web-resource-collection>
  <auth-constraint>
    <role-name>friend</role-name>
  </auth-constraint>
</security-constraint>

<security-role>
  <role-name>friend</role-name>
</security-role>
```

Setting authentication method

Finally, the application needs to be told how the security credentials (usually, username and password) are to be sent with the SOAP message.

On HTTP transport, simple applications will likely specify credentials through HTTP headers, for instance using **HTTP Basic Authentication** (RFC 2617).

JBossWS comes with a *@WebContext* annotation, which can be used, on EJB3 endpoint classes to specify the authorization method as follows:

```
import org.jboss.ws.api.annotation.WebContext;
import org.jboss.ws.api.annotation.AuthMethod;

@WebContext(authMethod = AuthMethod.BASIC)
@Stateless
@WebService
public class SecureEndpointImpl { . . . }
```

For POJO endpoints, instead, the *login-config* block of *web.xml* is to be used:

```
<login-config>
  <auth-method>BASIC</auth-method>
  <realm-name>Test Realm</realm-name>
</login-config>
```

 Username and password are sent as plaintext in a HTTP header when using HTTP Basic Authentication. Hence a secure implementation requires a secure connection to be established using SSL/TLS, which will be covered later in the chapter.

Client side credentials specification

On client side, users can specify the username and password for the invocation using the JAX-WS API and its **javax.xml.ws.BindingProvider** interface which allows storing credentials as key/value property pairs:

```
import javax.xml.ws.BindingProvider;
import javax.xml.ws.Service;

Service service = Service.create(wsdlURL, qname);
SecureEndpoint port = service.getPort(SecureEndpoint.class);

BindingProvider bp = (BindingProvider)port;
bp.getRequestContext().put(BindingProvider.USERNAME_PROPERTY, "kermit");
bp.getRequestContext().put(BindingProvider.PASSWORD_PROPERTY, "thefrog");
```

Transport level security on WildFly

The most common way of dealing with the above-mentioned security principles is possibly to rely on a secure transport. For Web Services running on the HTTP protocol, that basically means establishing a secure SSL connection, using the HTTPS protocol. Different containers come with different HTTP connector / listener configuration. WildFly allows setting up secure connections by editing the *standalone.xml* descriptor (as usual, the same can be achieved using either the command line interface or the web console). Securing connections is broken in two steps as described by the following sections:

Configuring the Security Realm

In order to enable HTTPS connections you need to create at first a keystore. If you need to perform a mutual authentication (where also the client provides a certificate), you need to create a truststore as well on client side.

Creating Server and Client Certificates

For this purpose, we will use the keytool utility that is part of the J2SE distribution. As first step, generate a public/private key pair for the entity whose alias is "serverkey" and has a "distinguished name" with a common name of "*Server Administrator*", organization of "*Acme*" and two-letter country code of "*GB*".

```
keytool -genkeypair -alias serverkey -keyalg RSA -keysize 2048 -validity 7360 -keystore
server.keystore -keypass mypassword -storepass mypassword -dname "cn=Server
Administrator,o=Acme,C=GB"
```

Now, if you want mutual SSL authentication generate a key pair also for the client, using the alias clientkey and registering a common name for it as well:

```
keytool -genkeypair -alias clientkey -keyalg RSA -keysize 2048 -validity 7360 -keystore
client.keystore -keypass mypassword -storepass mypassword -dname "cn=Desktop
user,o=Acme,C=GB"
```

Next, we will export both the server's and client's public key into a certificate named respectively **server.crt** and **client.crt**:

```
keytool -export -alias serverkey -keystore server.keystore -rfc -file server.crt -keypass
mypassword -storepass mypassword
```

```
keytool -export -alias clientkey -keystore client.keystore -rfc -file client.crt -keypass
mypassword -storepass mypassword
```

Now in order to successfully complete the SSL handshake, we need at first to import the client's public key into server's truststore:

```
keytool -import -file server.crt -keystore client.truststore -keypass mypassword -storepass
mypassword
```

The keytool will dump the certificate on your terminal and ask if it is has to be considered trustworthy.

```
Trust this certificate? [no]:  y
```

Answer yes and move on. As a final step, the server certificate too needs to be trusted. Therefore, we will import it into the client truststore:

```
keytool -import -file client.crt -keystore server.truststore -keypass mypassword -storepass
mypassword
```

Again, state that you are going to trust the certificate. Well done, you have completed the certificate installation. Now copy the server keystore and truststore files into a folder reachable by the application server. For example its configuration folder:

```
C:\tmp>copy server.keystore C:\wildfly-8.1.0.Final\standalone\configuration
C:\tmp>copy server.truststore C:\wildfly-8.1.0.Final\standalone\configuration
```

Defining a Security Realm on WildFly

Next step will be declaring a **Security Realm** to be used by the listener that will later be added. Hence, open your WildFly configuration file (e.g. *standalone.xml/domain.xml*) and include a new security realm under *server/management/security-realms*.

```
<security-realm name="test-https-realm">
  <server-identities>
    <ssl>
        <keystore path="server.keystore"
                  relative-to="jboss.server.config.dir"
                  keystore-password="mypassword" alias="serverkey"/>
    </ssl>
  </server-identities>
  <authentication>
            truststore path="server.truststore"
            relative-to="jboss.server.config.dir"
```

113

```
                    keystore-password="mypassword"/>
   </authentication>
</security-realm>
```

In the example above, *test-https-realm* specifies:

1. A server identity, which is defined by the certificate stored under the *"serverkey"* alias in the referenced *server.keystore*;

2. A truststore (*server.truststore*) to be used for authenticating clients.

Configuring the Undertow listener

The web functionalities of WildFly application server are provided by the Undertow subsystem. In the corresponding section of the *standalone.xml*, we have highlighted the listener that needs to be added to the server configuration:

```
<subsystem xmlns="urn:jboss:domain:undertow:1.0">

  ...
  <server name="default-server">
    <http-listener name="default" socket-binding="http"/>
    <https-listener name="test-https-listener" socket-binding="https" security-realm="test-
https-realm" verify-client="REQUESTED"/>
    <host name="default-host" alias="localhost">
      <location name="/" handler="welcome-content"/>
      <filter-ref name="server-header"/>
      <filter-ref name="x-powered-by-header"/>
    </host>
  </server>

  ...
</subsystem>
```

An *https-listener* with name *"test-https-listener"* is declared; it references the *security-realm* created above and requires client identity verification (*verify-client="REQUESTED"*). It also references the *"https"* socket binding, which is already defined in the default configuration, later in the *socket-binding-group* of the *standalone.xml*.

Setting transport guarantee

After having prepared the application server to support the HTTPS protocol, the Web Services application needs to be adapted to use it. That is achieved by setting a proper **security constraint** in the application *web.xml* (war deployments).

```xml
<web-app
    version="2.5" xmlns="http://java.sun.com/xml/ns/javaee"
    xmlns:xsi="http://www.w3.org/2001/XMLSchema-instance"
    xsi:schemaLocation="http://java.sun.com/xml/ns/javaee
http://java.sun.com/xml/ns/javaee/web-app_2_5.xsd">
    <servlet>
        <servlet-name>TestService</servlet-name>
        <servlet-class>...</servlet-class>
    </servlet>
    <servlet-mapping>
        <servlet-name>TestService</servlet-name>
        <url-pattern>/*</url-pattern>
    </servlet-mapping>
    <security-constraint>
      <web-resource-collection>
        <web-resource-name>TestService</web-resource-name>
        <url-pattern>/*</url-pattern>
      </web-resource-collection>
      <user-data-constraint>
        <transport-guarantee>CONFIDENTIAL</transport-guarantee>
      </user-data-constraint>
    </security-constraint>
</web-app>
```

Please note the *transport-guarantee*, which is set to *CONFIDENTIAL* to tell the container HTTPS connections are to be used.

In case of EJB3 based endpoints, a convenient JBossWS annotation can be used instead on the endpoint class:

```
@org.jboss.ws.api.annotation.WebContext(transportGuarantee="CONFIDENTIAL",
secureWSDLAccess="true")
```

The *secureWSDLAccess* attribute tells the container whether the published endpoint contract is to be secured as well or made publicly available. In any case, the generated endpoint addresses in the published WSDL contract will use the https protocol. The application server will as well accept https invocations only, on the port defined in *standalone.xml* for the *socket-binding* in use (by default 8443).

Client side configuration

Finally, in order for a Web Services client to communicate with an endpoint running on a secure HTTPS connection, the client environment needs to be properly set; a bunch of system properties control the way the underlying JDK connection is established:

Property	Description
javax.net.ssl.trustStore	Location of the client truststore
javax.net.ssl.trustStorePassword	Password of the client truststore
javax.net.ssl.trustStoreType	Type of the client truststore
javax.net.ssl.keyStore	Location of the client keystore
javax.net.ssl.keyStorePassword	Password of the client keystore
javax.net.ssl.keyStoreType	Type of the client keystore

The keystore is meant to contain a single certificate only. The properties can be set when starting the virtual machine or programmatically as follows:

```
System.setProperty("javax.net.ssl.trustStore", "my.truststore");
System.setProperty("javax.net.ssl.trustStorePassword", "changeit");
System.setProperty("javax.net.ssl.trustStoreType", "jks");
System.setProperty("javax.net.ssl.keyStore", "my.keystore");
System.setProperty("javax.net.ssl.keyStorePassword", "changeit");
System.setProperty("javax.net.ssl.keyStoreType", "jks");
```

Any JAX-WS client running in a virtual machine configured above will be able to invoke an endpoint running on HTTPS protocol, as the underlying JAX-WS implementation of WildFly uses the JDK HTTP Connection which in turn relies on such properties.

Alternatively, you can make direct use of **Apache CXF** API for setting up the HTTP transport, bypassing the default JDK mechanism. That is achieved getting the CXF **HTTPConduit** from the CXF Client, which in turn is retrieved by the JAX-WS client port instance through the **ClientProxy** utility class. Here is an example of it:

```
import org.apache.cxf.endpoint.Client;
import org.apache.cxf.frontend.ClientProxy;
import org.apache.cxf.transport.http.HTTPConduit;
import org.apache.cxf.configuration.jsse.TLSClientParameters;
...
Client client = ClientProxy.getClient(port);
HTTPConduit conduit = (HTTPConduit) client.getConduit();
TLSClientParameters parameters = new TLSClientParameters();
//setup parameters
conduit.setTlsClientParameters(parameters);
```

The *TLSClientParameters* class allows controlling any low level SSL configuration option.

WS-Security

Transport level security, covered in the previous section of this chapter, is a good solution for ensuring authenticity and confidentiality when exchanging SOAP messages over HTTP. However, there are some scenarios in which HTTP-based security is not enough. Complex applications may be sending messages using a more complex paradigm than request/response or over a transport that does not involve HTTP (such as JMS, UDP, whatever).

The point-to-point security provided by HTTPS does not suit multiple hops message exchanges, while a full end-to-end security solution is needed. **WS-Security** provides such a solution by putting together and leveraging few existing security standards and specifications; the most notable ones are:

- XML Signature, for signing messages

- XML Encryption, for encrypting messages
- X.509 for relying on public keys and certificates
- XML canonicalization, for properly comparing XML fragments

WS-Security includes information about the message issuer (identity) and how it was signed / encrypted through specific **SOAP headers** contained into the SOAP message.

A message secured through WS-Security can thus be safely sent over any insecure transport protocol.

WS-SecurityPolicy

While the WS-Security specification defines the way for securing SOAP messages (by means of SOAP headers), it does not tell anything regarding the WSDL contract for the endpoint that is going to process such messages.

Describing the security mechanisms to be used for a given endpoint advertised in a given WSDL contract is a **WS-SecurityPolicy** specification concern.

The WS-SecurityPolicy is an extension to the **WS-Policy** framework specification; it defines policy assertions covering the security binding (symmetric / asymmetric), the XML encryption algorithm to use, the signature / encryption ordering, the security token to include in messages, etc.

By looking at a WS-SecurityPolicy enabled contract, a Web Services client is able to figure out how to build a WS-Security message that the server will be successfully processing. At the same time, the server will be enforcing the rules specified in the contract assertions, rejecting messages that are not compliant with them.

Apache CXF implementation and WildFly

The WildFly / JBossWS support for WS-Security is based on the underlying Apache CXF and **Apache WSS4J** implementation of WS-Security and WS-SecurityPolicy.

The suggested approach for configuring a WS-Security enabled endpoint is to rely on WS-SecurityPolicy additions to the WSDL (contract-first development). This approach ensures good interoperability and requires just few configuration items to be dealt with. As a matter of fact, there are some mandatory configuration elements that are not covered by the WS-SecurityPolicy, basically because they're not meant to be public / part of the published endpoint contract; those include things such as keystore locations, usernames and passwords, etc. Apache CXF allows configuring these elements either through Spring XML descriptors or using the client API / annotations. Below is the list of the most common configuration properties:

Property	Description
ws-security.username	The username used for UsernameToken policy assertions
ws-security.password	The password used for UsernameToken policy assertions. If not specified, the callback handler will be called.
ws-security.callback-handler	The Apache WSS4J security CallbackHandler that will be used to retrieve passwords for keystores and UsernameTokens.
ws-security.signature.properties	The property file/object that contains the Apache WSS4J properties for configuring the signature keystore and crypto objects
ws-security.encryption.properties	The property file/object that contains the Apache WSS4J properties for configuring the encryption keystore and crypto objects
ws-security.signature.username	The username or alias for the key in the signature keystore that will be used. If not specified, it uses the default alias set in the properties file. If that's also not set, and the keystore only contains a single key, that key will be used.
ws-security.encryption.username	The username or alias for the key in the encryption keystore that will be used. If not specified, it uses the default alias set in the properties file. If that's also not set, and the keystore only contains a single key, that key will be used. For the WS provider, the *useReqSigCert* keyword can be used to encrypt any client whose public key is in the service's truststore.

The property files to be used for signature and encryption options are Apache WSS4J plain text configuration files using a standard *[key=value]* format like the following one:

```
org.apache.ws.security.crypto.provider=org.apache.ws.security.components.crypto.Merlin
org.apache.ws.security.crypto.merlin.keystore.type=jks
org.apache.ws.security.crypto.merlin.keystore.password=password
org.apache.ws.security.crypto.merlin.keystore.alias=bob
org.apache.ws.security.crypto.merlin.keystore.file=bob.jks
```

This file provides information to access the keystores needed to get keys and certificates for signature and encryption.

Client side configuration

The above-mentioned properties can be easily set in the request context using the plain JAX-WS API:

```
Map<String, Object> ctx = ((BindingProvider)port).getRequestContext();
ctx.put("ws-security.encryption.properties", "META-INF/alice.properties");
ctx.put("ws-security.signature.properties", "META-INF/alice.properties");
...
port.echo("hi");
```

Server side configuration

On server side, instead, endpoints can be configured through Apache CXF annotations, such as the **@EndpointProperty** annotation

```
@WebService(
    wsdlLocation = "WEB-INF/wsdl/SecurityService.wsdl", //WS-SecurityPolicy enriched WSDL
)
@EndpointProperties(value = {
  @EndpointProperty(key = "ws-security.signature.properties", value = "bob.properties"),
  @EndpointProperty(key = "ws-security.encryption.properties", value = "bob.properties"),
  @EndpointProperty(key = "ws-security.signature.username", value = "bob"),
  @EndpointProperty(key = "ws-security.encryption.username", value = "alice"),
  @EndpointProperty(key = "ws-security.callback-handler", value =
"org.foo.MyKeystorePasswordCallback")
    })
public class ServiceEndpointImpl {    ... }
```

Alternatively, the JBossWS integration allows declaring the properties within an *endpoint configuration,* referenced through the *@EndpointConfig* annotation:

```
import org.jboss.ws.api.annotation.EndpointConfig;

...
@WebService(
    ...
  wsdlLocation = "WEB-INF/wsdl/SecurityService.wsdl", //WS-SecurityPolicy enriched WSDL
    ...
)
@EndpointConfig(configFile = "WEB-INF/jaxws-endpoint-config.xml", configName = "Custom WS-
Security Endpoint")
public class ServiceEndpointImpl {
    ...
}
```

An example of *jaxws-endpoint-config.xml* file containing WS-Security Endpoint properties follows here:

```
<?xml version="1.0" encoding="UTF-8"?>
<jaxws-config xmlns="urn:jboss:jbossws-jaxws-config:4.0"
xmlns:xsi="http://www.w3.org/2001/XMLSchema-instance"
  xmlns:javaee="http://java.sun.com/xml/ns/javaee" xsi:schemaLocation="urn:jboss:jbossws-
jaxws-config:4.0 schema/jbossws-jaxws-config_4_0.xsd">
  <endpoint-config>
    <config-name>Custom WS-Security Endpoint</config-name>
    <property>
      <property-name>ws-security.signature.properties</property-name>
      <property-value>bob.properties</property-value>
    </property>
    <property>
      <property-name>ws-security.encryption.properties</property-name>
      <property-value>bob.properties</property-value>
    </property>
    <property>
      <property-name>ws-security.signature.username</property-name>
      <property-value>bob</property-value>
```

```
    </property>
    <property>
      <property-name>ws-security.encryption.username</property-name>
      <property-value>alice</property-value>
    </property>
    <property>
      <property-name>ws-security.callback-handler</property-name>
      <property-value>org.foo.MyKeystorePasswordCallback</property-value>
    </property>
  </endpoint-config>
</jaxws-config>
```

The next sections of this chapter show some real world examples of Web Services applications making use of WS-Security and WS-SecurityPolicy.

Signature and encryption example

The *wsse-sign-encrypt-sample* project is an example scenario where the message exchange is encrypted and integrity protected by means of X.509 certificates (and public key pairs); As mentioned above, the suggested approach for dealing with WS-Security scenarios is provide a contract definition (WSDL) first, also known as *top-down* Web Services. That might be complex and time consuming, so a little trick has been used to save time and bother manually writing only the policy section of the contract:

1. The previously introduced *jaxws-codefirst* Maven archetype is used to generated a bottom-up project skeleton

2. The project is built, deployed and tested (*mvn widfly:deploy; mvn integration-test; mvn wildfly:undeploy*)

3. The generated WSDL contract and the corresponding XSD schema are copied over to the *src/main/resources/WEB-INF/wsdl* directory and manually modified to add the desired WS-Security Policy section

4. The new WSDL is referenced in the endpoint implementation class

5. The *wsprovide* plugin invocation is removed from the *pom.xml* and the location of the WSDL file (that the *wsconsume-test* plugin has to consume) is changed to the generated one.

This way, the project is easily converted into a code-first one. The WS-Security options have to be properly set, then it will be executed and tested. Let's see what changes have been applied in detail, assuming you have successfully completed Step 1 and 2.

Server side configuration

As discussed in **Step 3** of the above bullet list, the following **WS-SecurityPolicy** has been added to the new WSDL file:

```
<wsp:Policy wsu:Id="SecurityServiceEncryptThenSignPolicy" xmlns:sp="http://docs.oasis-open.org/ws-sx/ws-securitypolicy/200702">
    <wsp:ExactlyOne>
      <wsp:All>
          <sp:AsymmetricBinding xmlns:sp="http://docs.oasis-open.org/ws-sx/ws-securitypolicy/200702">
            <wsp:Policy>
              <sp:InitiatorToken>
                <wsp:Policy>
                    <sp:X509Token sp:IncludeToken="http://docs.oasis-open.org/ws-sx/ws-securitypolicy/200702/IncludeToken/AlwaysToRecipient">
                      <wsp:Policy>
                        <sp:WssX509V1Token11/>
                      </wsp:Policy>
                    </sp:X509Token>
                </wsp:Policy>
              </sp:InitiatorToken>
              <sp:RecipientToken>
                <wsp:Policy>
                    <sp:X509Token sp:IncludeToken="http://docs.oasis-open.org/ws-sx/ws-securitypolicy/200702/IncludeToken/Never">
                      <wsp:Policy>
                        <sp:WssX509V1Token11/>
                      </wsp:Policy>
                    </sp:X509Token>
                </wsp:Policy>
              </sp:RecipientToken>
```

```
        <sp:AlgorithmSuite>
          <wsp:Policy>
            <sp:TripleDesRsa15/>
          </wsp:Policy>
        </sp:AlgorithmSuite>
        <sp:Layout>
          <wsp:Policy>
            <sp:Strict/>
          </wsp:Policy>
        </sp:Layout>
        <sp:IncludeTimestamp/>
        <sp:ProtectTokens/>
        <sp:OnlySignEntireHeadersAndBody/>
        <sp:EncryptBeforeSigning/>
      </wsp:Policy>
    </sp:AsymmetricBinding>
    <sp:SignedParts xmlns:sp="http://schemas.xmlsoap.org/ws/2005/07/securitypolicy">
      <sp:Body/>
    </sp:SignedParts>
    <sp:EncryptedParts xmlns:sp="http://schemas.xmlsoap.org/ws/2005/07/securitypolicy">
      <sp:Body/>
    </sp:EncryptedParts>
    <sp:Wss10 xmlns:sp="http://schemas.xmlsoap.org/ws/2005/07/securitypolicy">
      <wsp:Policy>
        <sp:MustSupportRefIssuerSerial/>
      </wsp:Policy>
    </sp:Wss10>
    </wsp:All>
  </wsp:ExactlyOne>
</wsp:Policy>
```

Asymmetric binding is specified, as well as some few assertions to control the algorithm suite to use and various security aspects like signature and encryption order, inclusion of timestamps, the sections of the message to protect (header and body), etc.

The security policies described in this book are meant to provide examples and directions to allow understanding how to configure WS-Security. Please note the implementer remains responsible for assessing the application requirements and choosing the most suitable security policy for them.

As last step, the SecurityServiceEncryptThenSignPolicy has then to be referenced in the proper WSDL *binding* element through a *PolicyReference* tag:

```
<wsdl:binding name="HelloWorldServiceSoapBinding" type="tns:HelloWorld">
    <wsp:PolicyReference URI="#SecurityServiceEncryptThenSignPolicy"/>
    ...
</wsdl:binding>
```

Moving on to **Step 4**, the new contract is specified in the *@WebService* annotation on the endpoint implementation class:

```
import javax.jws.WebService;
import javax.jws.soap.SOAPBinding;
import javax.jws.soap.SOAPBinding.Style;
import javax.jws.soap.SOAPBinding.Use;
import org.jboss.ws.api.annotation.EndpointConfig;

@WebService(endpointInterface = "com.itbuzzpress.HelloWorld",
            targetNamespace = "http://hello.world.ns/",
            name = "HelloWorld",
            serviceName = "HelloWorldService",
            portName = "HelloWorldPort",
            wsdlLocation = "WEB-INF/wsdl/HelloWorldService.wsdl")
@SOAPBinding(style = Style.DOCUMENT, use = Use.LITERAL)
@EndpointConfig(configFile = "WEB-INF/jaxws-endpoint-config.xml", configName = "Custom WS-
Security Endpoint")
public class HelloWorldImpl implements HelloWorld {

    ...

}
```

As you can see, the **@EndpointConfig** annotation is also being used to tell the container the *"Custom WS-Security Endpoint"* configuration from the *WEB-INF/jaxws-endpoint-config.xml* descriptor has to be assigned to the endpoint. Such file is added in the *src/main/resources/WEB-INF* directory and looks as follows:

```xml
<?xml version="1.0" encoding="UTF-8"?>

<jaxws-config xmlns="urn:jboss:jbossws-jaxws-config:4.0"
xmlns:xsi="http://www.w3.org/2001/XMLSchema-instance"
xmlns:javaee="http://java.sun.com/xml/ns/javaee"

  xsi:schemaLocation="urn:jboss:jbossws-jaxws-config:4.0 schema/jbossws-jaxws-
config_4_0.xsd">

  <endpoint-config>

    <config-name>Custom WS-Security Endpoint</config-name>

    <property>

      <property-name>ws-security.signature.properties</property-name>

      <property-value>bob.properties</property-value>

    </property>

    <property>

      <property-name>ws-security.encryption.properties</property-name>

      <property-value>bob.properties</property-value>

    </property>

    <property>

      <property-name>ws-security.signature.username</property-name>

      <property-value>bob</property-value>

    </property>

    <property>

      <property-name>ws-security.encryption.username</property-name>

      <property-value>alice</property-value>

    </property>

    <property>

      <property-name>ws-security.callback-handler</property-name>

      <property-value>com.itbuzzpress.KeystorePasswordCallback</property-value>

    </property>

  </endpoint-config>

</jaxws-config>
```

The specified properties basically set the callback handler for accessing the keystores and link to the *bob.properties* WSS4J property file (when dealing with keys and certificates in the example here, "bob" is used for the server and "alice" for the client).

The *bob.properties* file is put in ***src/main/resources/WEB-INF/classes*** dir, together with the *bob.jks* keystore and is as simple as:

```
org.apache.ws.security.crypto.provider=org.apache.ws.security.components.crypto.Merlin
org.apache.ws.security.crypto.merlin.keystore.type=jks
org.apache.ws.security.crypto.merlin.keystore.password=password
org.apache.ws.security.crypto.merlin.keystore.alias=bob
org.apache.ws.security.crypto.merlin.keystore.file=bob.jks
```

The **KeystorePasswordCallback** handler class, on the other hand, provides the passwords to be used for getting keys and certificates from the keystore:

```java
import java.util.HashMap;
import java.util.Map;
import org.jboss.wsf.stack.cxf.extensions.security.PasswordCallbackHandler;

public class KeystorePasswordCallback extends PasswordCallbackHandler {
    public KeystorePasswordCallback() {
        super(getInitMap());
    }
    private static Map<String, String> getInitMap() {
        Map<String, String> passwords = new HashMap<String, String>();
        passwords.put("alice", "password");
        passwords.put("bob", "password");
        return passwords;
    }
}
```

The WS-Security configuration on server side is ready; in order to allow building the endpoint archive properly, the *pom.xml* generated by the Maven archetype has to be tuned a bit (**Step 5**).

- At first, we need to perform some changes in the *maven-war-plugin* configuration. The following highlighted *webResources* block is needed to make sure that the descriptors mentioned above are included in proper locations within the target war archive:

```
<plugin>
    <artifactId>maven-war-plugin</artifactId>
    <version>2.4</version>
    <configuration>
     <webResources>
        <resource>
           <directory>src/main/resources</directory>
        </resource>
     </webResources>
       <archive>
          <manifestEntries>
            <Dependencies>org.jboss.ws.cxf.jbossws-cxf-client</Dependencies>
          </manifestEntries>
       </archive>
    </configuration>
</plugin>
```

- As you can see, within the *maven-war-plugin* configuration we have also included a **JBoss Module dependency** to the *org.jboss.ws.cxf.jbossws-cxf-client* module, because of the WSS4J usage and the callback handler class; that is achieved by adding a *Dependencies* entry in the deployment MANIFEST.MF.

- Finally, within the *pom.xml*'s resources, the *WEB-INF* project resources have to be filtered so that the descriptors do no end up being duplicated in the archive:

```
<build>
  ...
  <resources>
    <resource>
      <directory>src/main/resources</directory>
      <excludes>
```

```
        <exclude>WEB-INF/**</exclude> <!-- Exclude WEB-INF as it's treated in the war
plugin -->
      </excludes>
    </resource>
  </resources>
</build>
```

At this point, the war archive can be deployed to the server with the usual *mvn clean; mvn wildfly:deploy* command. WildFly will deploy the HelloWorldImpl endpoint, whose published WSDL contract can be seen at http://localhost:8080/wsse-sign-encrypt-sample/HelloWorldService?wsdl .

Client side configurations

As a client to the deployed endpoint, we'll modify and use the *com.itbuzzpress.HelloWorldIntegrationTest* that's generated by the Maven archetype.

Before any call to the HelloWorld interface methods, the port has to be configured to add the WS-Security related properties to the request context:

```
Map<String, Object> ctx = ((BindingProvider)port).getRequestContext();

ctx.put(SecurityConstants.CALLBACK_HANDLER, new KeystorePasswordCallback());
ctx.put(SecurityConstants.SIGNATURE_PROPERTIES,
Thread.currentThread().getContextClassLoader().getResource("alice.properties"));
ctx.put(SecurityConstants.ENCRYPT_PROPERTIES,
Thread.currentThread().getContextClassLoader().getResource("alice.properties"));
ctx.put(SecurityConstants.SIGNATURE_USERNAME, "alice");
ctx.put(SecurityConstants.ENCRYPT_USERNAME, "bob");
```

The values for the properties are symmetrical to those we specified on server side. The references *alice.properties* file is added to *src/test/resources* directory (together with the *alice.jks* keystore) and looks as simple as:

```
org.apache.ws.security.crypto.provider=org.apache.ws.security.components.crypto.Merlin
org.apache.ws.security.crypto.merlin.keystore.type=jks
org.apache.ws.security.crypto.merlin.keystore.password=password
org.apache.ws.security.crypto.merlin.keystore.alias=alice
org.apache.ws.security.crypto.merlin.keystore.file=alice.jks
```

For the sake of simplicity, the *KeystorePasswordCallback* is the same class used on server side; usually you'd have separate classes, as the keystores would come from different organizations and have different passwords.

To complete the project and allow running the test client, a final change to the generated *pom.xml* is required; to make the properties file and the keystore available to the client, they have to be included in the general **test resources**; filtering has to be disable for such resources, as that can result in corrupted keystore files:

```
<build>
  ...
  <testResources>
    ...
    <testResource>
      <directory>src/test/resources</directory>
      <filtering>false</filtering> <!-- disable filtering to avoid corrupting the keystore
-->
      <includes>
        <include>**/*.jks</include>
        <include>**/*.properties</include>
        <include>**/*.xml</include>
      </includes>
    </testResource>
  </testResources>
  ...
</build>
```

At this point, the client can eventually be run, through the *mvn integration-test* command.

The client will be retrieving the endpoint WSDL, figure out that WS-Security is required to invoke it, prepare the message, sign, encrypt it, and eventually send it. The server will decrypt, validate and process the request, eventually replying with another encrypted and signed message, that the client will in turn process again and return the contents of in the JAX-WS client within the testcase.

The following sequence diagram depicts the steps discussed so far, showing how the JAX-WS Client communicates with the Server in a secure manner through a Client proxy:

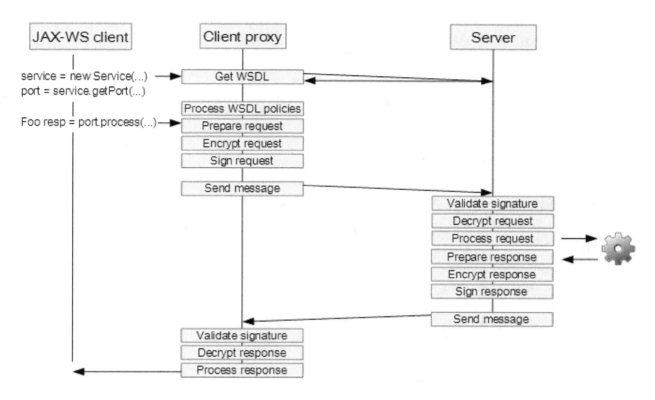

Authentication and authorization example

In the next example, named *wsse-auth-sample*, **explicit authentication and authorization** are required. This use case corresponds to the situation where both parties have X.509 certificates (and public-private key pairs).

The initiator includes a user name token that may stand for the requestor on-behalf-of which the initiator is acting. The *UsernameToken* is included as a *SupportingToken*, which is also encrypted. Additionally, on server side the username token is going to validated leveraging the JAAS integration, that is by delegating the authentication and authorization to the WildFly security layer. Finally, an EJB3 based endpoint is going to be used, so that you can easily rely on annotations to set permission requirements.

The project is generated from scratch the same way as the previous one (*wsse-sign-encrypt-sample*) was; in addition to the same changes to *pom.xml* described before, a dependency to *org.jboss.ejb3:jboss-ejb3-ext-api* artifact is added, to allow using the **@SecurityDomain** annotation:

```
<dependency>
  <groupId>org.jboss.ejb3</groupId>
  <artifactId>jboss-ejb3-ext-api</artifactId>
  <version>2.1.0</version>
  <scope>provided</scope>
</dependency>
```

WildFly configuration

As the WS endpoint of the application will be delegating authentication and authorization to the WildFly security layer, a proper security domain has to be created and configured. The *standalone.xml* file has been configured as follows:

```
<security-domain name="TestWS">
  <authentication>
    <login-module code="UsersRoles" flag="required">
      <module-option name="usersProperties" value="/foo/wildfly-8.0.0.Final/testws-users.properties"/>
      <module-option name="unauthenticatedIdentity" value="anonymous"/>
      <module-option name="rolesProperties" value="/foo/wildfly-8.0.0.Final/testws-roles.properties"/>
    </login-module>
  </authentication>
</security-domain>
```

The *testws-users.properties* in turn contains the following user definition:

```
kermit=thefrog
```

On the other hand, here is the *testws-roles.properties*:

```
kermit=friend
```

This basically tells the container we want a security domain configured to use a login module aware of a single *"kermit"* user with password *"thefrog"* and assigned the *"friend"* role.

Server side configuration

The endpoint WSDL contract is modified the same way as the previous example, except for a different policy, named **SecurityServicePolicy**, which has been included:

```
<wsp:Policy wsu:Id="SecurityServicePolicy">
  <wsp:ExactlyOne>
    <wsp:All>
      <sp:AsymmetricBinding xmlns:sp="http://docs.oasis-open.org/ws-sx/ws-
securitypolicy/200702">
        <wsp:Policy>
          <sp:InitiatorToken>
            <wsp:Policy>
              <sp:X509Token
                sp:IncludeToken="http://docs.oasis-open.org/ws-sx/ws-
securitypolicy/200702/IncludeToken/AlwaysToRecipient">
                <wsp:Policy>
                  <sp:WssX509V1Token11/>
                </wsp:Policy>
              </sp:X509Token>
            </wsp:Policy>
          </sp:InitiatorToken>
          <sp:RecipientToken>
            <wsp:Policy>
              <sp:X509Token
                sp:IncludeToken="http://docs.oasis-open.org/ws-sx/ws-
securitypolicy/200702/IncludeToken/Never">
                <wsp:Policy>
                  <sp:WssX509V1Token11/>
                </wsp:Policy>
              </sp:X509Token>
            </wsp:Policy>
          </sp:RecipientToken>
          <sp:AlgorithmSuite>
            <wsp:Policy>
              <sp:Basic128/>
            </wsp:Policy>
```

```xml
                    </sp:AlgorithmSuite>
                    <sp:Layout>
                        <wsp:Policy>
                            <sp:Strict/>
                        </wsp:Policy>
                    </sp:Layout>
                    <sp:IncludeTimestamp/>
                    <sp:OnlySignEntireHeadersAndBody/>
                </wsp:Policy>
            </sp:AsymmetricBinding>
            <sp:SignedParts xmlns:sp="http://schemas.xmlsoap.org/ws/2005/07/securitypolicy">
                <sp:Body/>
            </sp:SignedParts>
            <sp:EncryptedParts xmlns:sp="http://schemas.xmlsoap.org/ws/2005/07/securitypolicy">
                <sp:Body/>
            </sp:EncryptedParts>
            <sp:Wss10 xmlns:sp="http://schemas.xmlsoap.org/ws/2005/07/securitypolicy">
                <wsp:Policy>
                    <sp:MustSupportRefIssuerSerial/>
                </wsp:Policy>
            </sp:Wss10>
            <sp:SignedEncryptedSupportingTokens xmlns:sp="http://docs.oasis-open.org/ws-sx/ws-securitypolicy/200702">
                <wsp:Policy>
                    <sp:UsernameToken
                        sp:IncludeToken="http://docs.oasis-open.org/ws-sx/ws-securitypolicy/200702/IncludeToken/AlwaysToRecipient">
                        <wsp:Policy>
                            <sp:WssUsernameToken10/>
                        </wsp:Policy>
                    </sp:UsernameToken>
                </wsp:Policy>
            </sp:SignedEncryptedSupportingTokens>
        </wsp:All>
```

```
  </wsp:ExactlyOne>
</wsp:Policy>
```

In the above mentioned policy file, an *AsymmetricBinding* assertion (similar to the previous sample) has been included; besides that, a *SignedEncryptSupportingTokens* assertion is also specified, in order to have an username token included in the message (signed and encrypted). The token brings the username/password to the recipient, so that the user can be identified, authenticated and authorized.

The *HelloWorldImpl* endpoint class is enriched with few more annotations:

```
import javax.annotation.security.RolesAllowed;
import javax.ejb.Stateless;
import javax.jws.WebService;
import javax.jws.soap.SOAPBinding;
import javax.jws.soap.SOAPBinding.Style;
import javax.jws.soap.SOAPBinding.Use;
import org.apache.cxf.interceptor.InInterceptors;
import org.jboss.ejb3.annotation.SecurityDomain;
import org.jboss.ws.api.annotation.EndpointConfig;
import org.jboss.ws.api.annotation.WebContext;


@Stateless
@WebService(... ,wsdlLocation = "WEB-INF/wsdl/HelloWorldService.wsdl")
@SOAPBinding(style = Style.DOCUMENT, use = Use.LITERAL)
@EndpointConfig(configFile = "WEB-INF/jaxws-endpoint-config.xml", configName = "Custom WS-
Security Endpoint")
@SecurityDomain("TestWS")
@WebContext(urlPattern="/HelloWorldService")
@InInterceptors(interceptors =
{"org.jboss.wsf.stack.cxf.security.authentication.SubjectCreatingPolicyInterceptor"})
public class HelloWorldImpl implements HelloWorld {
    @RolesAllowed("friend")
    public Stringi sayHi(String text) { ... }
    @RolesAllowed("relative")
    public String greetings(Person person) { ... }
}
```

In particular, in addition to the usual *@WebService*, *@SOAPBinding* and *@EndpointConfig*, we have included:

- A **@Stateless** annotation, to declare the endpoint as stateless EJB3 endpoint instead of a POJO one

- A **@SecurityDomain** annotation, to have the container link the endpoint to the *"TestWS"* security domain for authentication and authorization

- A **@WebContext** declaration, to specify an explicit *urlPattern* to be used when computing the target endpoint address; this is actually optional, we have added it here just to have the endpoint published at the same address it would have been published if it was a POJO endpoint

- A **@InInterceptor** CXF annotation which is used to add the JBossWS *SubjectCreatingPolicyInterceptor* to the CXF interceptor chain; this is basically the hook for having CXF delegate the security subject creation (which is related to authentication and authorization) to JBossWS and hence WildFly

- **@RolesAllowed**, standard annotations to restrict endpoint business methods to users associated to the specified roles.

The referenced ***jaxws-endpoint-config.xml*** descriptor looks as follows:

```xml
<?xml version="1.0" encoding="UTF-8"?>

<jaxws-config xmlns="urn:jboss:jbossws-jaxws-config:4.0"
xmlns:xsi="http://www.w3.org/2001/XMLSchema-instance"
xmlns:javaee="http://java.sun.com/xml/ns/javaee"

  xsi:schemaLocation="urn:jboss:jbossws-jaxws-config:4.0 schema/jbossws-jaxws-
config_4_0.xsd">

  <endpoint-config>

    <config-name>Custom WS-Security Endpoint</config-name>

    <property>

      <property-name>ws-security.signature.properties</property-name>

      <property-value>bob.properties</property-value>

    </property>

    <property>

      <property-name>ws-security.encryption.properties</property-name>

      <property-value>bob.properties</property-value>
```

```
    </property>
    <property>
      <property-name>ws-security.signature.username</property-name>
      <property-value>bob</property-value>
    </property>
    <property>
      <property-name>ws-security.encryption.username</property-name>
      <property-value>useReqSigCert</property-value>
    </property>
    <property>
      <property-name>ws-security.callback-handler</property-name>
      <property-value>com.itbuzzpress.KeystorePasswordCallback</property-value>
    </property>
    <property>
      <property-name>ws-security.validate.token</property-name>
      <property-value>false</property-value>
    </property>
  </endpoint-config>
</jaxws-config>
```

The changes in properties compared to the previous sample are:

- *ws-security.validate.token*, which is set to **false** and basically instructs Apache CXF to skip the username token validation, as that is delegated to the container by the addition of the *SubjectCreatingPolicyInterceptor* mentioned before.

- *ws-security.encryption.username*, which is set to the special value *"useReqSigCert"*; this causes Apache CXF to encrypt the response message using the public key that was successfully used for verifying the request message signature. This is a mechanism for dynamically supporting multiple clients on server side, as long as their public key is known (registered in the server keystore). It's actually optional here (*"alice"* value would have worked too).

The *KeystorePasswordCallback* is the same as the previous sample; generally speaking, it's meant to be used for storing username / password pairs for the supported entries in the keystore (e.g. bob and alice). The endpoint application is eventually built the usual way through Maven. The container has to be modified to add the *TestWS* security domain before deploying the application; otherwise, it will fail because of unsatisfied dependencies.

Client side configuration

This time, the *HelloWorldIntegrationTest* generated by the Maven archetype is modified as follows:

```java
public class HelloWorldIntegrationTest {
    @Test
    public void testHelloWorld() throws Exception {
        HelloWorldService service = new HelloWorldService(new
URL("http://localhost:8080/wsse-auth-sample/HelloWorldService?wsdl"));
        HelloWorld port = service.getHelloWorldPort();
        setupWSSecurity(port);
        Assert.assertEquals("Hello Kermit", port.sayHi("Kermit"));
        Person p = new Person();
        p.setName("Anne");
        p.setSurname("Li");
        setupWSSecurity(port);
        try {
            port.greetings(p);
            Assert.fail("Authorization exception expected!");
        } catch (Exception e) {
            Assert.assertTrue("Authorization error message expected, but got: " +
e.getMessage(), e.getMessage().contains("not allowed"));
        }
    }
    private void setupWSSecurity(HelloWorld port) {
        Map<String, Object> ctx = ((BindingProvider)port).getRequestContext();
        ctx.put(SecurityConstants.CALLBACK_HANDLER, new ClientPasswordCallback());
        ctx.put(SecurityConstants.SIGNATURE_PROPERTIES,
Thread.currentThread().getContextClassLoader().getResource("alice.properties"));
        ctx.put(SecurityConstants.ENCRYPT_PROPERTIES,
Thread.currentThread().getContextClassLoader().getResource("alice.properties"));
        ctx.put(SecurityConstants.SIGNATURE_USERNAME, "alice");
        ctx.put(SecurityConstants.ENCRYPT_USERNAME, "bob");
```

```
            ctx.put(SecurityConstants.USERNAME, "kermit");
    }
}
```

By calling the *setupWSSecurity* method, we are setting an additional *SecurityConstants.USERNAME* entry to *"kermit"* in the request context; that is the user to specify in the UsernameToken. The password, which is still to be included in the token, is retrieved using the *ClientPasswordCallback* class; this class also includes the usual passwords for accessing the keystore:

```
import java.util.HashMap;
import java.util.Map;
import org.jboss.wsf.stack.cxf.extensions.security.PasswordCallbackHandler;

public class ClientPasswordCallback extends PasswordCallbackHandler {
    public ClientPasswordCallback() {
        super(getInitMap());
    }
    private static Map<String, String> getInitMap() {
        Map<String, String> passwords = new HashMap<String, String>();
        passwords.put("alice", "password");
        passwords.put("bob", "password");
        passwords.put("kermit", "thefrog");
        return passwords;
    }
}
```

As a result, the *testHelloWorld* method is going to hit an authorization exception when trying to invoke the greetings operation, as the endpoint will be requiring a *"relative"* role, which the *"kermit"* user is not assigned.

The rest of the project is the same as the previous *wsse-sign-encrypt-sample* one.

Upon running *mvn integration-test*, the client will be sending two signed and encrypted messages to the endpoint, both containing a username token with the *kermit* user credentials. The first request will succeed, while the second with cause an authorization exception error message to be returned to the client; both requests are anyway still encrypted and signed.

In order to pass the authentication check, triggered by the *greetings* method, you have to include the relative role in the *testws-roles.properties*:

```
kermit=friend,relative
```

Appendix

Across this book, we have intentionally used a neutral approach as far as it concerns the environment for developing Web Services. Since a large part of Java EE coders actually use the Eclipse platform for creating and testing Web Services, in the appendix of this book we will detail how to use Eclipse's Web Service wizard for this purpose.

In order to run our samples, you need to install some Eclipse plugins contained in the JBoss Tools projects (http://tools.jboss.org/) . The simplest way to do that, is to select from the **Help** menu **Eclipse Market Place** and enter the word "**JBoss tools**" in the search box:

Since we will use JBossWS for generating the Web Service artifacts, in the following screen, check the **JBoss Web Services** option along with the **JBossAS Tools**. The latter option will let you control JBoss AS and WildFly application servers from within the Eclipse UI.

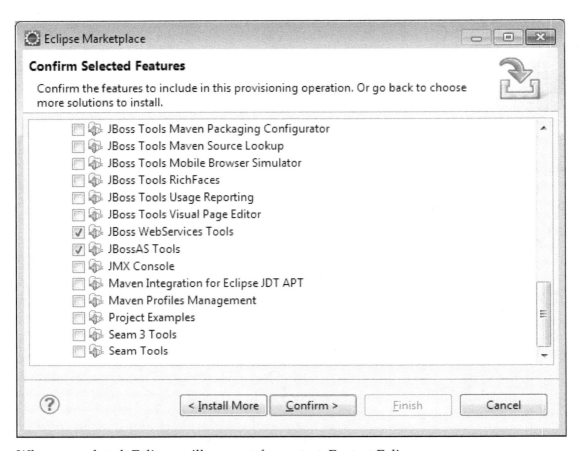

When completed, Eclipse will prompt for restart. Restart Eclipse.

Now we need to perform some steps, which are required to be done just once. At first, you need to define a new **Server** Runtime, hence from the File menu select **New** | **Other** and choose **Server**. In the Server UI, pickup your JBoss or WildFly application server, as displayed by the following window:

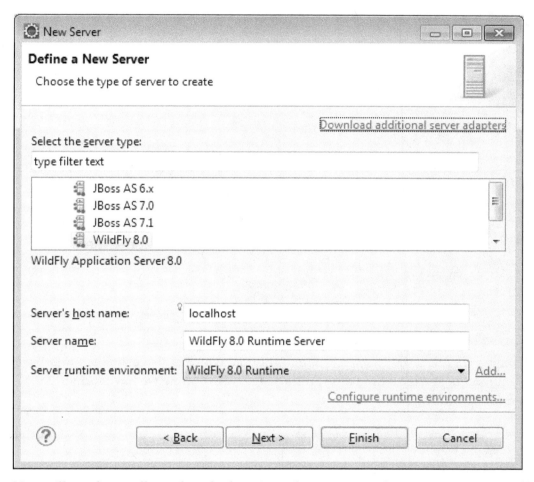

You will need as well to select the location where your application server is installed. When done, click on finish.

Next, we need to inform Eclipse about the location where the **JBossWS** runtime is located. The location of the JBossWS corresponds to the home of your JBoss/WildFly application server. Select **Window | Preferences**. In the preferences screen, expand the Web Services left option and select **JBoss WS Preferences**. There, you can choose the location of your JBossWS runtime. As displayed by the following picture, enter your JBOSS_HOME:

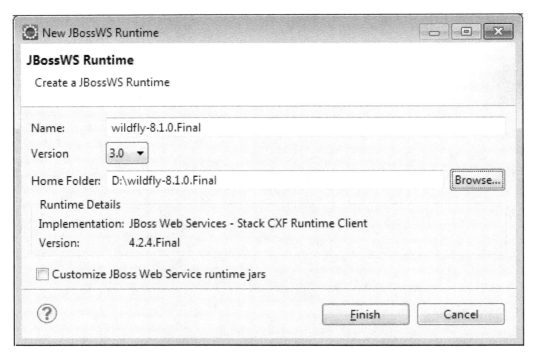

While still in the Preferences UI, select the "Server Runtime" option, which is also contained into the "Web Services" label. There, choose as Runtime the application server runtime we have formerly created and as Web Services Runtime "JBossWS":

Now you can start your Eclipse environment and create a new **Dynamic Web project** from the **File** Menu. Name your project for example **ws-demo-wsdl-1.0**

As first step, we need to enable the **JBoss Web Services Facet** from the Project **Properties** window, as displayed by the following picture:

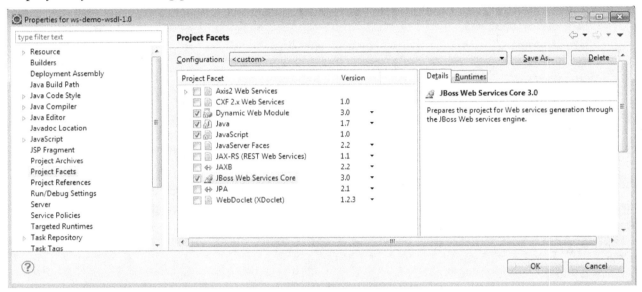

Once done, we are ready to create our Web Services. At first, include a WSDL in your project. You can reuse for this purpose the **CustomerService.wsdl** that has been discussed in Chapter 2 of this book.

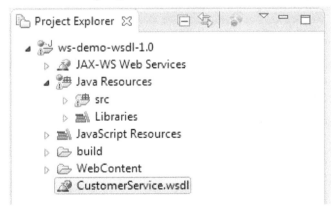

Now we will generate a Web Service based on this WSDL. Select from the File Menu the option **New** | **Other** | **Web Service**. In the upper ComboBox, specify to create a Web Service using the **top-down**

Web Service type and point to the *CustomerService.wsdl* file. Select as well **JBossWS** as Web Service runtime:

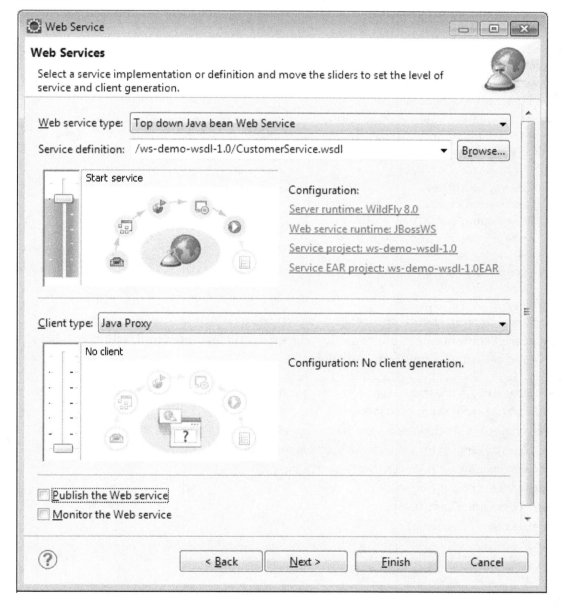

Right now, we will not generate a Web Service client, as we will use the **Web Tester UI** to test our Web Service. Click on **Finish**. From the Project explorer of Eclipse you will see that the following artifacts have been generated in your project:

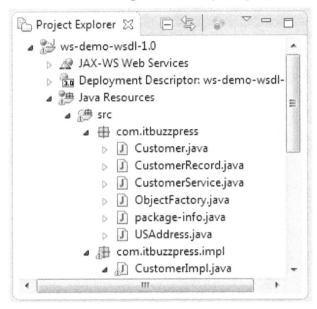

As you can see, the project contains an implementation class named **CustomerImpl,** which needs to be completed in order to return a value to our test client:

```java
@WebService(serviceName = "CustomerService", endpointInterface =
"com.itbuzzpress.Customer", targetNamespace = "http://wsdemo.chapter2.itbuzzpress.com/")
public class CustomerImpl implements Customer {
    public CustomerRecord locateCustomer(java.lang.String firstName,
                java.lang.String lastName, USAddress address) {
        CustomerRecord c = new CustomerRecord();
        c.setAddress(new USAddress());
        c.setFirstName(firstName);
        c.setLastName(lastName);
        return c;
    }
}
```

Now we can finally test our project: start at first the application server and publish the generated projects (the Web Service wizard has generated also an EAR wrapper for your Web project)

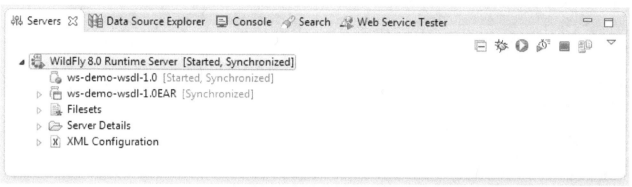

Verify on the console (http://localhost:9990) that the Web Service has been correctly registered:

Available Web Service Endpoints

▲ Name	Context	Deployment
com.itbuzzpress.chapter2.wsdemo.CustomerPortImpl	ws-demo-wsdl-1.0	ws-demo-wsdl-1.0.war

«   ‹   1-1 of 1   ›   »

Selection

Name:	com.itbuzzpress.chapter2.wsdemo.CustomerPortImpl
Context:	ws-demo-wsdl-1.0
Class:	com.itbuzzpress.chapter2.wsdemo.CustomerPortImpl
Type:	JAXWS_JSE
WSDL Url:	http://localhost:8080/ws-demo-wsdl-1.0/CustomerService?wsdl
Deployment:	ws-demo-wsdl-1.0.war

Now, from the Window menu select **Show view** | **Other** and choose **Web Service Tester view**. The Web Service tester UI will be appear.

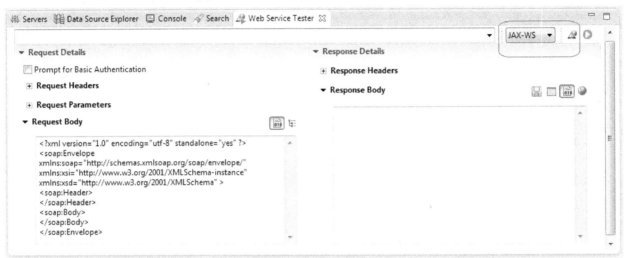

Select **JAX-WS** from the upper combobox and click on the nearby **Get From WSDL** button which will collect a sample Request Body based on the WSDL. Before that, you will have to specify in the next UI the location of the WSDL and the Service,Port and Operation as shown here:

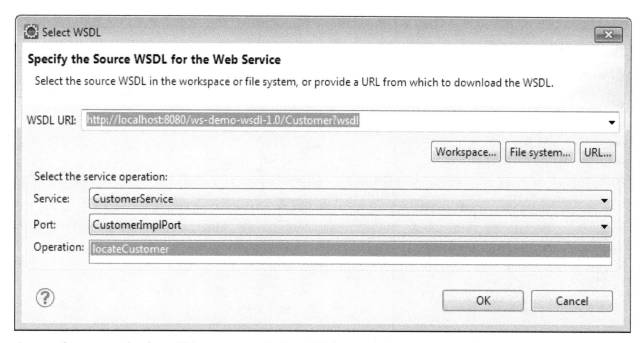

A sample request body will be generated. Just fill the Web Service parameters and click on the upper right **Invoke** button:

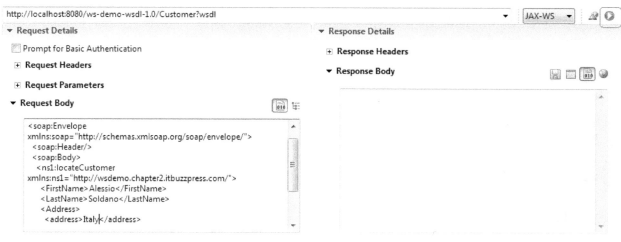

The expected result, based on our simple endpoint implementation, is an echo of the parameters that you have entered in the request:

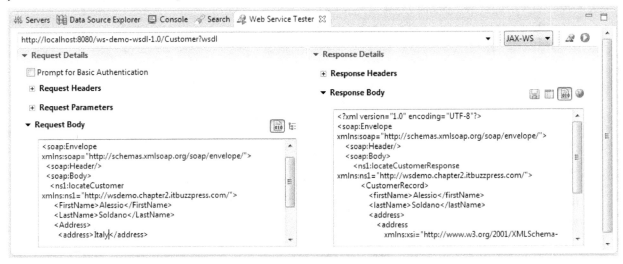

www.ingramcontent.com/pod-product-compliance
Lightning Source LLC
LaVergne TN
LVHW082347060326
832902LV00016B/2701